HUMBLE

Is the Way

McDougal & Associates

Servants of Christ and stewards of the mysteries of God

HUMBLE
Is the Way

by

David Jones

All Scripture quotations are from the
Authorized King James Version of the Bible.

Published by:

McDougal & Associates
P.O. Box 194
Greenwell Springs, LA 70739-0194
www.thepublishedword.com

McDougal & Associates is dedicated to the spreading of the Gospel of
Jesus Christ to as many people as possible in the shortest time possible.

ISBN 13: 978-0-9777053-6-8
ISBN 10: 0-9777053-6-6
Printed in the United States of America
For Worldwide Distribution

DEDICATION

This book is dedicated with love
to the entire House of Praise family.

ACKNOWLEDGMENTS

Special thanks to my wife, Suzie Jones, who has consistently stood by my side. To my secretary, Blanca Skok, for bearing the load with such efficiency and dedication. To my friend, Lunetta Broome, for her enthusiasm about the book and her sacrificial efforts to get it off the ground. To my dear friend, Anthony Barnett, for making this book a reality.

Contents

FOREWORD BY
PASTOR WALLY HAMILTON

I believe that Pastor David has captured the true heart of God concerning humility in his book, *Humble is the Way*. He masterfully outlines the causes and consequences of pride and arrogance, followed by the rewards and blessing of humility. I enjoyed his personal testimony concerning the struggle for humility in his own life. This book is a call to all believers to walk in humility and is so important that it should be required reading.

Pastor Wally Hamilton
Covenant Word Church
Webster, Texas

FOREWORD BY NATHAN WILLIAMS

It is my great privilege to lend my voice to the writings of Pastor David Jones. This is more than a book; it is a life experience, for it shows us how Pastor David has lived out the Word of God. All of us humans face challenges in life that place us in need of a Savior. God intervened early in Pastor David's life to save him from one of the most destructive forces in the universe—pride. Pastor David's story is very detailed, and he has, once again, humbled himself to tell it to us, so that others might be saved from the dangers he escaped.

I can truly say that Pastor David Jones is a very genuine Christian with a humble spirit, and I can easily see God promoting him in the near future to a much higher level. He has promises from God that will be fulfilled, and I believe he is a prepared vessel that will stand for the Lord and for His people in the days ahead.

This is not a trendy message but a necessary word that will stand the test of time. *Humble is the Way* applies to every living soul, but for the Christian, this message is not optional at all. There are many forces in life that can cause a Christian to become barren. Refusing to clothe ourselves in humility is one that brings automatic failure. Please invest in your life today by heeding the Word of God and delivering yourself from the weights of sin that so easily beset us all.

If you've been wanting to join the winners circle, *Humble is the Way* can point you in the right direction.

Nathan Williams
President, Jesus Is Mine Ministries
General Manager, Daystar Television Network

The fear of the Lord is the instruction of wisdom; and before honour is HUMILITY.   Proverbs 15:33

God resisteth the PROUD, but giveth grace unto THE HUMBLE. Submit yourselves therefore to God. Resist the devil, and he will flee from you.
HUMBLE YOURSELVES in the sight of the Lord, and he shall lift you up.   James 4:6-7 and 10

He that is the greatest among you shall be your servant. And whosoever shall exalt himself shall be abased; and he that shall HUMBLE HIMSELF shall be exalted.
Matthew 23:11-12

He hath shewed thee, O man, what is good; and what doth the LORD require of thee, but to do justly, and to love mercy, and to WALK HUMBLY with thy God?
Micah 6:8

PRIDE goeth before destruction, and an haughty spirit before a fall.   Proverbs 16:18

By HUMILITY and the fear of the Lord are riches, and honour and life.   Proverbs 22:4

An angry man stirreth up strife, and a furious man aboundeth in transgression. A man's PRIDE shall bring him low: but honour shall uphold THE HUMBLE in spirit.   Proverbs 29:22-23

For whosoever exalteth himself shall be abased; and he that HUMBLETH HIMSELF shall be exalted.

Luke 14:11

LORD, thou hast heard the desire of THE HUMBLE: thou wilt prepare their heart, thou wilt cause thine ear to hear.

Psalm 10:17

My soul shall make her boast in the Lord: THE HUMBLE shall hear thereof, and be glad.

Psalms 32:2

The LORD is nigh unto them that are of a broken heart; and saveth such as be of a CONTRITE spirit.

Psalm 34:18

The sacrifices of God are a broken spirit: a broken and a CONTRITE heart, O God, thou wilt not despise.

Psalm 51:17

For thus saith the high and lofty one that inhabiteth eternity, whose name is Holy; I dwell in the High and holy place, with him also that is of a CONTRITE AND HUMBLE spirit, to revive the spirit of THE HUMBLE, and to revive the heart of THE CONTRITE ones.

Isaiah 57:15

* Emphasis added

DEFINITIONS

Pride: A high or inordinate opinion of one's own dignity, importance, merit or superiority, whether as cherished in the mind or as displayed in bearing or conduct.

Proud: Conceited, exalted, lifted up in one's self.

Humility: The quality or condition of being humble.

Humble: (Noun) Not Proud or arrogant, courteously respectful. (Verb) To make meek, bring under subjection.

INTRODUCTION

To my way of thinking, nothing could be more important in life than humility—humility before God and humility before our fellowman. Humility before God is much more than bending your knees. Many do that, but it doesn't mean that they're humble. They're bending their bodies, but God wants to see their spirits bend.

Humility is the key to life. For sure, it's the key to our relationship with God (with everything that relationship entails), but it's also the key to other relationships: husband and wife, parents and children, employer and employee, pastor and member, commander and soldier, president and citizen, etc.

God says that He exalts the humble, and that alone should excite us all enough to make us want to learn more about this important subject. Humble yourself, and God will lift you up. It's as simple as that. And anytime you do the opposite, exalting yourself, you're headed for a fall. Pride never pays, and humility always does. What could be more simple?

As a pastor, I love to preach on many subjects, but this is one of the most important of our time. If any man or woman in any country of the world fails to learn humility, they will fall. Case closed! No appeal possible!

And if we're to accomplish anything at all in life, it will be done God's way. That requires humility, so I need more of it and so do you.

Interestingly enough, there are some sins for which God will show a person mercy, but pride is not one of them. When pride is present, He must deal with us quickly and severely, for He simply cannot tolerate pride.

The problem with many Christians is that they can quote the scriptures backwards and forwards, but it doesn't do them any good because they don't want to be humble. At least not this moment. Maybe later, but not now. And that's how the devil tricks us. We want to be humble, and we actually plan to be humble, but this current situation seems to demand that we exert ourselves and put people in their place. THEN, we'll be humble.

But when THEN comes, there's another situation that seems to demand that we stand strong and put people in their place, so humility gets put off until another day ... and another ... and another. Just when is the time to be humble? If it's not now, then when?

Somehow, when situations arise, and people offend us and do us wrong, it seems that we Christians don't really care what the Bible says in that moment. All we know is that we're determined to put the issues right, to put certain people in their place and to show who's right and who's wrong in the matter at hand. And when you do that, there's no grace for you; you're on your own. The Holy Ghost will leave you to your own devices. His grace is only for the humble, and in that moment you're not among them.

Much of this I learned the hard way and saw others learning the hard way—sometimes too late to avoid the consequences of their choices. As a result, I have taught extensively on this subject. Here, for the first time in print, is the best of the best of my teachings on humility. May the Spirit of the living God bless you as you read and give you grace to receive.

Pastor David Jones
House of Praise
Katy, Texas

PROLOGUE

For some years, I served as a lay person under a mighty bishop. His wisdom astounded me, and I sometimes felt that I was sitting under Solomon himself. When he told us what God was saying, I knew that I was in the presence of the Almighty. But when this man left the pulpit, he seemed to turn into a very different person. He was now quick tempered and short with the people around him, and I found this extremely difficult to deal with. It kept me on pins and needles all the time.

One day he said to me, "Brother Jones, would you be willing to help me with one of my rental properties? I'll pay you $10 an hour."

I was in between jobs at the time, so I didn't hesitate. "Yes, Sir!" I answered, and I showed up to work the next day.

It was a very hot day, I worked hard, and the sweat poured off of me. Still, when he came around to check on my progress, he said, "Now, Brother, I'm paying you good money, so you're going to have to pick it up."

I didn't say anything, but I also didn't see how I could work much faster. Still, I exerted even more effort and worked even harder.

Then, about ten minutes later, he came around again. "Brother, brother, brother, pick it up," he said, clearly irritated with my progress.

"What does this man want from me?" I wondered, not knowing how I could work any faster, and I started to get irritated with him.

"Bishop," I said, "do you know who you remind me of?"

"Who?" he asked.

"You remind me of my Daddy," I said. "If something wasn't done his way, it was never right—no matter what."

When I said that, a sudden silence fell over us. It was not just physical. It actually seemed to fall from Heaven itself.

He looked at me for what seemed the longest while, and then he said, "If you have any wisdom at all, you'll know that you've already said enough," and he turned away. But I already realized what I had done. My rebelliousness against authority had gotten me into trouble again.

This seemed to be the story of my life. Daddy had been harsh and overbearing, and to me at least, he often seemed totally unreasonable. When he died, I decided that no one would ever tell me what to do again, and by fourteen I was on my own, living in my own apartment and making my own decisions in life. This put me at odds with every authority figure in my life, got me kicked out of school, made my time in the Marines rather unbearable and spoiled most of my personal relationships.

But then, miracle of miracles, I had gotten saved, and now I was a Christian and was supposed to be different. It had taken me a while to begin learning submission to others, but it came, and I vowed to fully submit to God and to anyone He placed over my life. How else could I hope to prosper?

But what had gotten into me now that I had given in to a passing anger and had dared to judge and criticize this great man of God? This was a serious mistake that could have serious consequences. I'd seen it too many times. I had to make this right somehow.

"Please forgive me," I urged the Bishop. "I don't know what got into me. I should never have said that. I do know better."

"I'll forgive you," he said, "but God heard it too," and that seemed to be the end of it ... or was it?

The next morning, when I woke up, I was paralyzed from the neck down. I was all alone, and I was totally helpless. It was to be one of the darkest days of my life. I was due at work that morning, but I never made it. Instead I had an unexpected appointment with God.

Before long I wet on myself, but there was nothing I could do. I lay there all day long pleading with God to be merciful to me for what I had done and to heal me. If He did, I would go back to the bishop and apologize again, and I would never repeat this mistake—ever.

For hours, the heavens seemed to be brass, but I was desperate and continued to cry out to God. I had no choice. My entire future was in question.

Then, along about seven that evening, relief came, and I could move normally again. I quickly dressed and went out to see the bishop and ask his forgiveness. "I've already forgotten about that," he said.

"But I haven't," I insisted. "I couldn't, and I needed to do this." He understood and accepted my apology.

I tell this story at the beginning of this book, precious reader, so that you will know that when I speak about the need for humility, I know what I'm talking about. My flesh fought me for many years on this subject, and my mouth got me into trouble many times. But what I suffered taught me.

God requires humility of us, humility toward Him, humility toward His servants and humility toward the people in our daily lives—spouses, children, bosses, co-workers and even neighbors. When that humility is not forthcoming, He has to resort to other measures to humble us. And no one can chasten us like God can. He knows just how to reach us where it hurts most. Sometimes no one else is able to get our attention, but He can do it every time.

I learned the hard way to humble myself and have respect for God's servants—whether they were right or whether they were wrong. It was not my business to be rebuking or correcting them. God could do that well without my help.

That, then, is the background for the message of this book, that I trust will change your life, as it has changed mine.

I know that mine may be an extreme case, and I'm not saying that this is what will happen to you. What I am saying is that God is serious about our need for humility—toward Him and toward others.

PART I

PRIDE AND ITS
TERRIBLE CONSEQUENCES

CHAPTER 1

LUCIFER'S MISCALCULATION

How art thou fallen from heaven, O Lucifer, son of the morning! how art thou cut down to the ground, which didst weaken the nations! For thou hast said in thine heart, I will ascend into heaven, I will exalt my throne above the stars of God: I will sit also upon the mount of the congregation, in the sides of the north: I will ascend above the heights of the clouds; I will be like the most High. Yet thou shalt be brought down to hell, to the sides of the pit.   Isaiah 14:12-15

Early in biblical history, a precedent was set regarding pride and its consequences, and surprisingly, it took place, not on Earth at all, but in the heavens. All of us Christians are trying to get to Heaven, but Lucifer was already there. He was not only there; he had a prominent position there in God's presence. He was a special angel. The Scriptures describe him as he then was:

Thou sealest up the sum, full of wisdom, and perfect in beauty. Thou hast been in Eden the garden of God;

every precious stone was thy covering, the sardius, topaz, and the diamond, the beryl, the onyx, and the jasper, the sapphire, the emerald, and the carbuncle, and gold: the workmanship of thy tabrets and of thy pipes was prepared in thee in the day that thou wast created. Thou art the anointed cherub that covereth; and I have set thee so: thou wast upon the holy mountain of God; thou hast walked up and down in the midst of the stones of fire. Thou wast perfect in thy ways from the day that thou wast created.

Ezekiel 28:12-15

LUCIFER WAS "PERFECT"

It would be difficult to imagine a more beautiful and exalted creature than Lucifer was. Clearly, he was the most beautiful angel in Heaven, and God had made him that way. He was *"perfect"* in his ways from the day he was created.

This word *perfect* is not one the Bible uses lightly or often. Although Jesus urged all believers to strive for perfection, the Scriptures make clear that none is perfect but God Himself. Usually, when the Scriptures speak of the possibility of perfection for man, the word means more *maturity* than it does *perfection* as we know it. Still, Lucifer was *"perfect"* and had been *"perfect"* since he was created by God.

But this all changed one day, suddenly and dramatically, and it happened in a moment's time. It all changed because of a thought that entered into Lucifer's heart. I purposely left out the final words of verse 15, because I wanted you to first see his state before his fatal miscalculation. The final words of verse 15 declare ominously:

Thou wast perfect ... till iniquity was found in thee.
Ezekiel 28:15

AT THIS POINT, EVERYTHING CHANGED

> *There was a point in Lucifer's existence when everything changed!*

There was a point in Lucifer's existence when everything changed. Until that moment, he had been an exalted, respected and honored angel, one who stood by the Father's side and administered His will among other angels. In the next moment, he was suddenly *"fallen,"* *"cut down."* It was in that fateful moment that this once exalted angel became Satan, archenemy of God and of man, God's crowning creation. And Lucifer, now Satan, has remained a hated and feared figure ever since.

What could have brought about such a dramatic change in a glorious angel? What could cause one who was so highly favored of God to be so quickly and decisively *"cut down."* We know that *"iniquity was found"* in him, but what was that *"iniquity,"* and why did it have such serious consequences?

Lucifer did not perform any rebellious act, and neither did he utter any seditious word. All he did was think something, and yet that mere thought was enough to seal his fate. And what was it that he thought? He *"said"* something *"in [his] heart."* He didn't even speak the words out loud, but that didn't matter because God heard it anyway, and because what he said was so dangerous and arrogant, God simply could not let it stand.

"I WILL"

What did Lucifer say in his heart? He said that he wanted to *"ascend into heaven"* and *"exalt [his] throne above the stars of God."* He wanted to *"sit also upon the mount of the congregation, in the sides of the north"* and *"ascend above the heights of the clouds."* In other words, he wanted to *"be like the most High."*

We know that Lucifer was something glorious to behold, he was wise and he was *"perfect"* in his own way, but he was *not* God. Only God was God, and Lucifer was so far below God that his thoughts of being like God or exalting his throne above the stars of God were beyond foolish. This was about as arrogant as any angel could possibly get. Lucifer was what he was only because a loving God had made him that way, and yet, here he was, allowing his beauty, wisdom and perfection to cause him to have false thoughts of grandeur. This was nothing more than filthy pride, and God had to cut it down immediately and without recourse. It could not be allowed to stand.

LUCIFER'S MISCALCULATION

God loved Lucifer, but He could not overlook this sin. These prideful thoughts could not be allowed to pass unanswered. He immediately cast Lucifer out of Heaven, without a trial and without legal representation. He was *"out."* Period! No questions asked and no excuses entertained!

OTHER ANGELS ALSO REBELLED

Surprisingly, Lucifer was not the only one to have such thoughts in Heaven, and he was also not the only one to be cast out of God's presence. John declared in his revelation:

> *And the great dragon was cast out, that old serpent, called the Devil, and Satan, which deceiveth the whole world: he was cast out into the earth, and his angels were cast out with him.* Revelation 12:9

The glorious Lucifer existed no more; now he was *"the great dragon," "that old serpent," "the Devil"* or *"Satan."* He had lost all of his former glory, and now there was nothing good about him at all. He was never again to be called Lucifer. He had other names, but they were all evil. Why? Because he had exalted himself against God, and therefore he must be *"cast out."*

And when Lucifer was cast out, with him went *"his angels."* Who were these other angels? We don't know their names, but we do know that they had the same thoughts as the former Lucifer did. They, too, had succumbed to pride, and in their pride, they had exalted themselves against the Creator and conspired with the rebellious Lucifer. Therefore they, too, must be *"cast out."*

How many other angels were there in this group? We don't know exactly, but we do know that it was a very large number. The angels, whom God originally created to stand before Him and serve Him, were quite numerous—to say the least. We know this from several biblical passages:

> *That's pretty bad, isn't it: getting thrown out of Heaven!*

A fiery stream issued and came forth from before him: thousand thousands ministered unto him, and ten thousand times ten thousand stood before him.   Daniel 7:10

And suddenly there was with the angel a multitude of the heavenly host praising God ... .   Luke 2:13

But ye are come unto mount Sion, and unto the city of the living God, the heavenly Jerusalem, and to an innumerable company of angels.   Hebrews 12:22

Angels were and are *"innumerable,"* and fully one third of them were cast out of Heaven on that fateful day. So what's one third of *"innumerable"*? We can't know the number because it's still *"innumerable."* The fallen were so many that they could not be numbered.

Imagine it! God, the great Creator, had carefully, thoughtfully and lovingly formed each of these creatures to be His personal servants. They were created to stand before Him and do His bidding. And now fully one third of them had to be forever banished. What a sad day this was for Heaven!

That's pretty bad, isn't it: getting thrown out of Heaven! But that's just what happened, and that's what pride will do every time—if it is not dealt with and decisively overcome.

The question is why? What would cause a glorious angel to make such a deadly miscalculation? The answer is that pride has a blinding effect. Despite the fact that he was a created being, and what is created could never be greater than the one who created it, pride actually made him believe that he could rise above God. It's just that powerful and just that deadly.

SATAN'S CURRENT ROLE

Lucifer was *"cast out"* of Heaven, so he lost all of his heavenly privileges. He no longer has the privilege of praising God, so, instead, he fights the people of God unmercifully. He works on you every day to make you proud. Why? He wants more company. He's not satisfied that a third of the angels in Heaven followed him. He wants even more followers. Somehow he's still deceived, and he still believes that he can overcome God and win more converts than the Almighty.

Satan, the former Lucifer, hates God, and he hates you, and he's determined to make you proud. The Scriptures warn us:

> *Be sober, be vigilant; because your adversary the devil, as a roaring lion, walketh about, seeking whom he may devour: whom resist stedfast in the faith.*
>
> 1 Peter 5:8-9

Your adversary is determined that you will fall into the same trap of pride that caused his downfall, and you must be equally determined that you will not. That's the importance of this message. Hear the Lord today: *Humble Is the Way*!

CHAPTER 2

SAUL'S TERRIBLE LOSS

And Samuel said to Saul, Thou hast done foolishly: thou hast not kept the commandment of the LORD thy God, which he commanded thee: for now would the LORD have established thy kingdom upon Israel for ever. But now thy kingdom shall not continue: the LORD hath sought him a man after his own heart, and the LORD hath commanded him to be captain over his people, because thou hast not kept that which the LORD commanded thee. 1 Samuel 13:13-14

Angels are not the only ones who have suffered the terrible effects of pride. Men of every age have succumbed to this evil, and the results have always been dreadful. One of the well documented biblical examples of a man who suffered terrible loss as a result of pride is the sad story of King Saul.

SAUL'S HUMBLE BEGINNINGS

As a young man, Saul had been humble and caring.

He was a large man, taller than the other men of his day, plus he was good looking. But these were not the reasons God chose him to be Israel's first king. It was, instead, his tender heart. In every way, he was *"a choice young man"*:

> *And he [Kish] had a son, whose name was Saul, a choice young man, and a goodly: and there was not among the children of Israel a goodlier person than he: from his shoulders and upward he was higher than any of the people.* 1 Samuel 9:2

> **Saul obeyed to the letter everything that he was told!**

The early accounts of Saul's life show him doing many good things. He was willing to go out searching for his father's lost asses. He was concerned that his father would worry when several days passed and he and a servant who accompanied him were unable to find the animals. He was willing to pursue the servant's suggestion that they consult a man of God who lived nearby in the hope that this man could tell them what they should do. He was concerned about bringing a proper offering to the man of God, and borrowed from his servant to do it. He was in the right place at the right time when Samuel came along to anoint a king for Israel. And, most of all, he replied humbly when he was told what was to be his destiny:

And Saul answered and said, Am not I a Benjamite,
of the smallest of the tribes of Israel? and my family
the least of all the families of the tribe of Benjamin?
wherefore then speakest thou so to me?

1 Samuel 9:21

Saul's Careful Obedience

Before Saul left for home, he received some very specific instructions from the prophet. It involved a number
of things that he was to do. He obeyed to the letter everything that he was told. Among the things Samuel told
Saul that day was this promise:

And the Spirit of the LORD will come upon thee, and
thou shalt prophesy with them [other prophets he would
meet along the way], and shalt be turned into another
man.   1 Samuel 10:6

Saul did not protest that he was not a prophet. He was
open to whatever God had in store for him. And it all
happened, just as Samuel said it would—because Saul
was so humble and so obedient.

What Happened to the Old Saul?

If Saul started out so humble and so obedient (and the
two go together), what happened to him along the way?
For one thing, the fact that he was a big man and good

35

looking may have worked against him over time. Satan will use anything he can to tempt us to be prideful. The people under Saul came to love and appreciate him, and their words of praise probably had a negative effect on him as time went on. It happens to many. It's wonderful to be loved and praised, and we all want that and need it, but it can be deadly—if it goes to our head. We can guard against it by always remembering our humble beginnings and Who it was that made us what we now are.

The fact that Saul was chosen from among all others to be king also must have worked negatively on his spirit over time. Leadership at any level has always seemed to present men (and women) with an open door for temptation, and Satan is always there to try to take advantage of it.

Saul Changed

Whatever the reasons, Saul eventually let pride enter into his heart. The proof is in his change of attitude toward the prophet of God.

On at least two occasions, Saul revealed what was now in his heart. One of those occasions was the one referred to in our theme verse. He had been told to destroy all of the Amalekites together with their animals, but he chose instead to hold back some men and some animals to use for his own purposes. On the second occasion, he was told by Samuel to wait for him at a certain place until he came to offer sacrifices for him and the nation. When Samuel didn't arrive immediately, Saul grew impatient and went in and made the sacrifices in question himself—something that was completely out of order for him, even though he was king.

These acts show us that Saul no longer respected the man of God, and this meant that he no longer respected God Himself. The result was that God could not let his attitude stand. His chosen king was now out of control and had to be stopped.

SAUL HATED DAVID

The day Samuel told Saul that the kingdom was to be taken from him, he also told him that God had prepared someone to replace him. That someone, of course, was David, the humble shepherd boy. He was the *"man after [God's] own heart."* But when God began to exalt David and to give him favor with the people of Israel, Saul hated it. He didn't want anyone else but himself to be loved or praised.

One day, after David had won a glorious victory for the people, the women of the nation broke out into spontaneous songs of victory, and what they sang just added fuel to the fire of Saul's rage:

And the women answered one another as they played, and said, Saul hath slain his thousands, and David his ten thousands. And Saul was very wroth, and the

saying displeased him; and he said, They have as-
cribed unto David ten thousands, and to me they have
ascribed but thousands: and what can he have more
but the kingdom? And Saul eyed David from that day
and forward.   1 Samuel 18:7-9

Saul was the king, and David was just a shepherd boy, so Saul had nothing to be jealous of. But his pride could not bear the praise these women were heaping upon David for his exploits in battle.

For his part, David loved Saul and was loyal to him, but over the coming months and years, Saul would many times try to kill the lad. And, despite the fact that he was chosen as the king's son-in-law and lived in the palace, David was forced to flee for his life. For years, Saul chased the younger man from place to place, trying to take his life. Always, God protected David.

DAVID LEFT ALL VENGEANCE WITH GOD

On several occasions, David had the king in his hands and could have executed vengeance upon him, but he refused. Knowing Saul's ruthlessness, David's men urged him to end the king's life, but David was firm in his resolve not to harm his father-in-law. At one point, he caught Saul sleeping in a cave and actually cut off part of his robe to let him know that he could have killed him and didn't. Even that act bothered David's conscience:

SAUL'S TERRIBLE LOSS

And it came to pass afterward, that David's heart smote him, because he had cut off Saul's skirt. And he said unto his men, The LORD forbid that I should do this thing unto my master, the LORD's anointed, to stretch forth mine hand against him, seeing he is the anointed of the LORD.

1 Samuel 24:5-6

How could David afford to take this attitude? It was because he was sure that God would deal with Saul in His own time and in His own way, and that's exactly what happened. Saul's reign eventually ended in disgrace, and he died on the battlefield. David didn't have to lay a finger on him.

When you insist on taking things into your own hands, you're saying, "God, move out of the way, and let me be god. Let me deal with this situation. Let me take care of this." It's a very dangerous attitude. Humility in every situation always proves best.

> *Saul's pride could not bear the praise the women were heaping upon David for his exploits in battle!*

David's Own Arrogance

In time, David himself sinned, and his sin was serious. He committed adultery with Bathsheba, a married woman, and then he had her husband placed in the heat of battle so that he would be killed. It was very wrong, and he knew it was very wrong—no matter who he was and no matter what he was trying to accomplish.

The amazing thing about Bathsheba's husband, Uriah the Hittite, was that he was loyal to David, as David had been loyal to Saul. When David called Uriah home from the front and gave him the opportunity to go spend the night with his wife, the loyal soldier could not do it. He felt that it wasn't fair for him to sleep in his own bed with his own wife when his men were in tents on the battlefield.

Given a second opportunity, he spent the night with the rest of David's servants. What a humble and good man he was! And how terrible that David ordered him to be placed in a position where he would be vulnerable! It was an arrogant thing to do, and David paid for it the rest of his life.

The Difference Between Saul and David

So why is David remembered for the good things he did and Saul remember only for the bad? When confronted with his sin, David repented and sought God's forgiveness. Saul, on the other hand, died proclaiming his innocence.

SAUL'S TERRIBLE LOSS

Humility does not necessarily indicate perfection, but God can forgive a humble man and teach him not to repeat his wrong, while a prideful man goes from bad to worse and too often dies prematurely. The message is clear: *Humble Is the Way!*

Chapter 3

Uzziah's Sudden Decline

Moreover Uzziah built towers in Jerusalem at the corner gate, and at the valley gate, and at the turning of the wall, and fortified them. Also he built towers in the desert, and digged many wells: for he had much cattle, both in the low country, and in the plains: husbandmen also, and vine dressers in the mountains, and in Carmel: for he loved husbandry.   2 Chronicles 26:9-10

It should not surprise us that kings have a problem with pride. Often, when a person is especially gifted and talented, they become lifted up. The problem didn't end with Saul and David. Another great king, King Uzziah, had the very same problem.

This Man Was So Very Gifted

This man was so very gifted, and his gifts brought him and the people he ruled into great prosperity. He was a great builder, a great planter, a great fruit grower and a great cattle raiser. He was also a great military leader:

Moreover Uzziah had an host of fighting men, that went out to war by bands, according to the number of their account by the hand of Jeiel the scribe and Maaseiah the ruler, under the hand of Hananiah, one of the king's captains. The whole number of the chief of the fathers of the mighty men of valour were two thousand and six hundred. And under their hand was an army, three hundred thousand and seven thousand and five hundred, that made war with mighty power, to help the king against the enemy. And Uzziah prepared for them throughout all the host shields, and spears, and helmets, and habergeons, and bows, and slings to cast stones. And he made in Jerusalem engines, invented by cunning men, to be on the towers and upon the bulwarks, to shoot arrows and great stones withal. And his name spread far abroad; for he was marvellously helped, till he was strong.

2 Chronicles 26:11-15

Wow! To say that this man was extremely gifted seems like an understatement. God was certainly good to him.

Like all of us, Uzziah should have continually remembered his beginnings, and he should have continually expressed thankfulness to God for where He had taken him. That would have assured that his God-given prosperity continued. Instead, Uzziah's gift became a problem for him, as often happens, and he made a serious and fatal mistake:

UZZIAH'S SUDDEN DECLINE

But when he was strong, his heart was lifted up to his destruction: for he transgressed against the LORD his God, and went into the temple of the LORD to burn incense upon the altar of incense. 2 Chronicles 26:16

When you're weak, it's normal to be humble, but when you become strong, look out! That's when the temptation toward pride hits hardest. Uzziah was now strong, and suddenly he decided to do something that he was not qualified or authorized to do. If you are to reach greatness and maintain your position of greatness, you have to know your place, and then you have to keep your place—no matter what else happens.

> *Uzziah should have continually remembered his beginnings!*

NOW UZZIAH MUST BE REPROVED

When Uzziah got out of line, a senior priest, with an escort of eighty other priests, went into the temple to remind him that he was now out of order. The priests were the only ones authorized to enter the temple and burn incense, so what the king had done was prideful and arrogant and wrong, and the priests loved him enough to tell him about it:

And Azariah the priest went in after him, and with him fourscore priests of the Lord, that were valiant men: and they withstood Uzziah the king, and said unto him, It appertaineth not unto thee, Uzziah, to burn incense unto the Lord, but to the priests the sons of Aaron, that are consecrated to burn incense: go out of the sanctuary; for thou hast trespassed; neither shall it be for thine honour from the Lord God.

2 Chronicles 26:17-18

Uzziah's Totally Inadequate Response to Reproof

Uzziah, despite the fact that he was king over the people, was rebuked in no uncertain terms, and this could have been his salvation. Sadly, though, this stern rebuke did not yield the desired result. What Uzziah did next showed exactly where his heart was. Rather than humble himself and seek forgiveness from God and man, as he should have done (and God would have forgiven him), he became angry.

This was more than God could permit, and His response to the king was immediate and harsh:

Then Uzziah was wroth, and had a censer in his hand to burn incense: and while he was wroth with the priests, the leprosy even rose up in his forehead before the priests in the house of the Lord, from beside the incense altar. And Azariah the chief priest, and all the priests, looked upon him, and, behold, he was leprous in his forehead, and they thrust him out from thence; yea, himself hasted also to go out, because the LORD had smitten him. And Uzziah the king was a leper unto the day of his death, and dwelt in a several house, being a leper; for he was cut off from the house of the LORD: and Jotham his son was over the king's house, judging the people of the land.   2 Chronicles 26:19-21

How foolish it was for the king to become angry with those who were trying to help him! These were *"valiant men"* and men of God. They were not his enemies in any sense of the word. Still, he rejected their wise and kind counsel. If you know you've done wrong, and someone chastens you, please thank them and don't get angry with them.

If someone tells you that there are some rattlesnakes just ahead of you, and you insist on going forward, you're a fool, and you deserve whatever you get.

GOD'S RESPONSE WAS SWIFT AND HARSH

This kind of pride brings a quick and decisive response from God. As we have seen, He cannot let it stand. The moment Uzziah became angry, rather than repent for what he had done, something started to happen in his physical body. Leprosy, an incurable and contagious disease, began to appear on his forehead. Again, that's an indication of how serious God takes pride and arrogance.

Uzziah didn't see what was happening to him, but the priests did, and they had no choice but to get the king out of the temple as quickly as possible and away from all the people. He was polluting that holy place and had to be physically removed.

> **King Uzziah was polluting that Holy place and had to be physically removed!**

At some point, Uzziah, too, realized what was happening, and he *"hasted to go out."* What had happened? Why was Uzziah now a leper? The Scriptures are clear: *"because the LORD had smitten him."* This was God's doing. He cannot stand pride and must deal with it harshly and immediately.

"CUT OFF"

"Cut off!" What terrible words! Believe me, you don't want to be *"cut off"* by God. So repent when you're wrong, humble yourself in His presence, and thus avoid His wrath. You cannot stand against God's wrath. Whatever you do, don't let anything cause you to be *"cut off from the house of the Lord."* That's a punishment worse than death.

Gifted and prosperous King Uzziah died as a leper, cut off from the house of the Lord, and his son had to make all the day-to-day decisions for the nation because his father could no longer do it.

UZZIAH'S SUDDEN DECLINE

THIS KIND OF STUBBORNNESS WILL GET YOU NOWHERE

Some people are so stubborn. They don't care what anyone says; they're going to do just what they want to do. No wonder they suffer so much! And they bring it all upon themselves through their pride and disobedience.

What a gifted man Uzziah had been! How brilliant! How blessed! And how foolish! He let it all go to his head, and the result was that he lost everything.

Again, it should not surprise us that kings have had a problem with pride. Often, when a person is especially gifted and talented, they become lifted up within themselves and start having confidence in their flesh. It doesn't just happen to a few; it happens to many. Pride is one of the most common sins—even among Christians, and it leads to many other sins and to eventual destruction—if it's not dealt with decisively.

What about you? God is getting you ready for greatness, and part of your preparation is to learn humility. Please learn to walk softly before Him today so that He can exalt you quickly.

For my part, I'm working on myself, crying out to God to help me humble myself and learn to walk ever so softly before Him. We don't want God to have to humble us. We want to learn humility on our own, for: *Humble Is the Way!*

❧

Chapter 4

Herod's Fateful Arrogance

*And upon a set day Herod, arrayed in royal apparel,
sat upon his throne, and made an oration unto them.
And the people gave a shout, saying, It is the voice of
a god, and not of a man. And immediately the angel
of the Lord smote him, because he gave not God the
glory: and he was eaten of worms, and gave up the
ghost. But the word of God grew and multiplied.*

Acts 12:21-24

When the Old Testament gave way to the New Testament, it was with sweeping changes.

The Old Gave Way to the New

The appearance of the Savior had made all the difference. Those who followed the New, although they were also Jews at the first, were called by a totally different name. They were Christians, because they were followers of the Christ, or Christlike. Suddenly, salvation was no longer obtained through the Law, but by faith in Christ

Himself. The Temple in Jerusalem suddenly lost its importance, for one Sacrifice had been made for every man for all time, and now everyone who believed in Christ became a temple fit for God's presence. One thing, however, did *not* change. God still could not tolerate pride and always had to deal with it quickly and severely—whether it was found in a king or in any other man or woman.

> *Herod Agrippa I was also sometimes called Herod the Great, and he loved it!*

WHO WAS THIS HEROD?

By this time, the kings over Israel served under a very different system. Palestine had become part of the Roman Empire, and the kings served at the will of the Caesars. Still, God could not tolerate pride in them. This is proved by what happened to Herod.

Incidentally, this was not the same Herod who was ruling at the time of the birth of Christ and had all the boy babies of Bethlehem under the age of two slaughtered to try to snuff out the life of the future King of the Jews. This was his grandson, Herod Agrippa I, son of Aristobulus IV and Berenice. It seems that he had inherited some of his grandfather's grandeur. Indeed, like his grandfather, he was also sometimes called Herod the Great, and he loved it.

HE "HAD IT GOING ON"

On a particular day, Herod was all dressed up in his finest, his *"royal apparel,"* and he sat on his throne, looking very much like the king that he was. From that position, he made a great speech, or, as the Bible calls it, an *"oration,"* to the people. In every way, we can see that this man "had it going on."

It must have been a powerful oration Herod gave that day, for when he had finished, the people began to shout and say that his was the voice of a god, not a man. Oh, how dangerous that was! Those were words that needed to be corrected immediately. No man is ever allowed to take God's glory, and Herod had been around the Jewish people long enough to know that. Still, he said nothing, for he was enjoying the moment too much to spoil it.

This Herod was already proud, and the sudden declaration of the people, that he had the voice of a god, just seemed to push him over the edge. And that could not be tolerated. Whatever God does, we must give *Him* the glory, for He will not share His glory with another—not then, not now and not ever. He has said:

I am the LORD: that is my name: and my glory will I not give to another, neither my praise to graven images.
Isaiah 42:8

Herod clearly had a problem, but it was the people who pushed him over the edge. And you have to watch the people around you. They will try every way they can to lift you up, and you can't afford to go along with them. Knowing that being lifted up is a sure recipe for a fall, you must reject people's applause. Instead, point them to Jesus. Cause them to give God glory, and not you. Don't receive their praise for yourself.

Depending on your position in life, people will tell you how anointed you are, how well you can preach or teach, how well you can sing, how great and wise you are or some other such thing. And when they do this, watch out! It's a setup for sure. They may not even know it, but they're just tools of the enemy in an attempt to get you to fall.

HEROD'S SILENCE CONDEMNED HIM TO DEATH

Herod should have known better, but he remained silent in this matter. He failed to give God the glory and, instead, accepted the praise for himself.

So what did God do? *"Immediately the angel of the Lord smote him [Herod] ... , and he was eaten of worms, and gave up the ghost."* When? *"Immediately"*! Why? *"Because he gave not God the glory!"* What? *"He was eaten of worms, and gave up the ghost!"*

For those who are not yet familiar with this biblical phrase, "give up the ghost," it means simply that he died. He died right there on the spot. He died in front of those people who were giving him their adulation.

HEROD'S FATEFUL ARROGANCE

When did he die? *"Immediately!"* Why did he die? *"Because he gave not God the glory!"* How did he die? *"He was eaten of worms."* What a horrible death! And it happened right there in the sight of all those people who had been praising Herod and causing him to be lifted up in pride.

Please don't ever allow people to puff *you* up. Always give God the glory due to His name.

You're getting ready to be blessed, and God is proving your heart, so that He will know who can be trusted. This is one area in which you simply must not fail.

I Determined Not To Let It Happen

I'm speaking from experience. Through the years, I've seen the damage praise can do to people, and I've tried to avoid it like the plague.

When I was still a young minister, I sometimes preached when my pastor was out of town, and the people of the church loved it. Later, as I was on my way to my car in the parking lot, some of them would shout out to me, "Hey, Bishop! Hey, Pastor! Hey, Apostle!"

"I'm not the pastor here!" I objected. "I'm just a minister, and I'm just filling in for a few days until Pastor gets back."

"Oh, you'll be the next pastor here," they said assuredly. "Soon enough, you'll be our next Apostle."

I said, "Would you stop that! Do you want to get me killed?" That's how serious I take this matter. It's no laughing, or joking, matter. This is a deadly serious business. I wasn't about to lose my blessing because of those people's ignorance.

Herod's punishment was swift and severe, and yours will be too, for God cannot tolerate pride. He simply can't do it, and don't expect Him to make an exception in your case. There are no exceptions when it comes to pride. If you currently have no fear of God in this respect, you'd better develop one quickly. A healthy fear of God is the beginning of wisdom and knowledge:

> *The fear of the LORD is the beginning of wisdom: a good understanding have all they that do his commandments: his praise endureth for ever.*   Psalm 111:10

> *The fear of the LORD is the beginning of knowledge: but fools despise wisdom and instruction.*
>   Proverbs 1:7

> *The fear of the LORD is the beginning of wisdom: and the knowledge of the holy is understanding.*
>   Proverbs 9:10

Oh, beloved, learn this lesson. For king or commoner alike, *Humble Is the Way!*

CHAPTER 5

ANANIAS' AND SAPPHIRA'S COSTLY MISTAKE

But a certain man named Ananias, with Sapphira his wife, sold a possession, and kept back part of the price, his wife also being privy to it, and brought a certain part, and laid it at the apostles' feet.   Acts 5:1-2

Some might believe that pride is a problem only for those who have never known Christ. I wish it were true, but it's not.

CAN CHRISTIANS BE PROUD?

Surely Christians can't be proud! Isn't this an Old Testament problem? Isn't this for worldly kings and other world rulers, for men and women of false cults and false religions and for those who purposely set themselves against God and against His teachings? Alas, Christians also struggle with pride. In fact, pride may well be our greatest struggle in the Christian life.

When you think about it, this makes sense. Satan is the author of pride, and he's not satisfied just to have the world exalted in pride against God. His real target is those of us who make up the Church, the sons and daughters of God. He already has the others in his grip, so we're the ones he now wants, and we have thus become his major targets.

An Early Example

Very early in New Testament history, there's a story of pride and its sad aftermath that is just as dramatic and powerful as any in the Old Testament, and it has to do with Christians. This story set the tone for things to come, for it let everyone know that God had not changed His mind about pride and its consequences. He still could not tolerate it—even when it was found within those who named His name. It was just as deadly in them as in those of the world. Maybe more so, because these people had much more to lose.

The story goes like this: At a time when many believers were looking for ways to finance the work of the early church, many of them selling excess properties and laying the money they derived from those sales at the feet of the apostles, there was a couple named Ananias and Sapphira. This couple, too, sold a property, and they, too, laid some money at the feet of the apostles. The difference was that they kept back part of the price and then conspired to lie about how much they had received for the sale of their property.

Now, why would they have done that? It was their property, and they could do with it what they wanted. The apostles were making no demands upon the people, and every offering was voluntary, so what was this couple's motivation to lie about what they were giving? The only answer can be pride. Ananias and Sapphira wanted everyone to think that they had done more than they actually had, and this prideful desire made them dare to lie to the apostles the Lord Jesus Himself had chosen to run His Church in the first century.

GOD WAS NOT FOOLED

God was not fooled for a minute by what this couple did, and neither were the apostles. Peter knew immediately that what Ananias was saying was a lie, and he confronted him about it:

> *God was not fooled for a minute by what this couple did, and neither were the apostles!*

> But Peter said, Ananias, why hath Satan filled thine heart to lie to the Holy Ghost, and to keep back part of the price of the land? Whiles it remained, was it not

thine own? and after it was sold, was it not in thine own power? why hast thou conceived this thing in thine heart? thou hast not lied unto men, but unto God.

Acts 5:3-4

Some ministers might have felt so grateful for any amount the couple had given that they would have refused to say anything that might have hurt their feelings. Far too often, money is the chief motivator in these cases. But Peter could not keep silent, because God could not keep silent, and Peter was God's servant.

By disrespecting God's servants, this man Ananias had offended God, and this could not be allowed to pass. Ananias and Sapphira had taken the apostles for fools and felt that they could easily deceive them, but they were wrong. These men may have come from a humble Galilean fishing background, but God was in them.

THE RESPONSE WAS QUICK AND SURE

Everyone quickly saw what the result of pride in the New Testament and among Christians was to be:

And Ananias hearing these words fell down, and gave up the ghost: and great fear came on all them that heard these things. And the young men arose, wound him up, and carried him out, and buried him.

Acts 5:5-6

ANANIAS' AND SAPPHIRA'S COSTLY MISTAKE

As before, God's answer to pride was immediate and severe, and that fact caused *"fear,"* as it should have. Why did the people suddenly *"fear"* God? Because they saw that His policy regarding pride and lifting oneself up against Him and His servants had not changed. He still hated pride, and He still could not tolerate it in any form. Ananias died right there in church in front of everyone, and that was a powerful lesson.

SAPPHIRA WAS ALSO JUDGED

In the meantime, Mrs. Ananias (or Sapphira, as she was called) was out spending some of the money they had held back, and so she didn't know what had happened to her husband. A few hours after he died, she came around, probably to receive what she considered to be her just thanks from the apostles for her gracious gift. She should have come back repenting and saying, "My husband and I did something wrong, and we must now make it right. We don't want to lose God's favor, so we must admit what we did and face the consequences." Instead, she came with the same old tired story, and therefore she was faced, not with praise, but with a serious and angry confrontation:

And it was about the space of three hours after, when his wife, not knowing what was done, came in. And Peter answered unto her, Tell me whether ye sold the land for so much? And she said, Yea, for so much. Then Peter said unto her, How is it that ye have agreed together to tempt the Spirit of the Lord? behold, the feet of them which have buried thy husband are at the door, and shall carry thee out.   Acts 5:7-9

Peter gave the woman the chance to repent and make things right. When he began asking specifically about the amount of the sale, why didn't she suspect that he was "on to" their trickery? She must have known that something was up. But, alas, pride would not allow her to back down. She and her husband had agreed on a certain lie, so now she must stick to that lie, although it seemed that Peter was somewhat suspicious of it.

> **Peter gave the woman the chance to repent and make things right!**

So, like her husband before her, Sapphira's fate was also sealed. She was now told that her husband had preceded her in death and had already been buried. And then those fateful words: the same men who had carried her husband to his grave would now come to carry her body away.

Did Sapphira have any time at all, even seconds, to consider the impact of those words? Did she have any time at all to think about the foolish thing she and her husband had done and what the terrible consequences were? Did she even have time to grieve the loss of her husband? It seems that she did not. She'd had her chance, and pride had caused her to refuse it. For a split second, she may have grieved her loss, and then she had to face an angry God. Her judgment was swift and sure:

> *Then fell she down straightway at his feet, and yielded up the ghost: and the young men came in, and found her dead, and, carrying her forth, buried her by her husband. And great fear came upon all the church, and upon as many as heard these things.*   Acts 5:10-11

FEAR IS WHAT OUR MODERN WORLD NEEDS

"Great fear came upon all the church, and upon as many as heard these things," and that's exactly what we need to happen again today in the church. Because New Testament history started in this way and the story of Ananias and Sapphira spread far and wide, the shock of it caused Christians everywhere to fear God and His servants and to do the right thing. As a result, their story was not repeated often in early church history.

Today, however, not only our world seems totally out of control. Our churches are out of control, as well. Our marriages are out of control. Our children are out of control. And the business world is out of control. And it's all because of pride and its terrible effects.

What must God do to correct this situation? Expect to hear soon about some Ananiases and some Sapphiras. He cannot remain silent, and we have no right to expect Him to stand back and do nothing about the situation.

"But isn't He a God of love?" Yes, He is, but He's also a God of judgment. What would our world be like without judgment and justice? And what would the eternal Church be without it? Let Ananias and Sapphira stand for all times as a sentinel of warning.

So the pattern is clear: Old Testament and New ... people of the world and people of the Church ... God cannot tolerate pride, and He must deal with it harshly. *Humble Is the Way!*

PART II

HUMILITY AND ITS GLORIOUS REWARDS

CHAPTER 6

NAAMAN'S TURNAROUND

Now Naaman, captain of the host of the king of Syria, was a great man with his master, and honourable, because by him the LORD had given deliverance unto Syria: he was also a mighty man in valour, but he was a leper.　　　　　　2 Kings 5:1

Not every Old Testament story ended sadly, as the story of Saul and Uzziah did, and not every New Testament story ended sadly, as the stories of Herod and Ananias and Sapphira did. Some men and women, when confronted with the need for humility, found it within themselves to respond positively, and their story, therefore, had a happy ending. Pride is not necessarily deadly. If it's recognized and repented of in time, then there's hope. Naaman of old was one of these exceptions.

A GREAT AND HONORABLE MAN HAD A PROBLEM

Naaman was a great and honorable man, a man of valor, but he had a problem. He was a leper, and that was worse than a death sentence. Having this terrible disease in those days resulted in complete isolation. As lepers neared other people, they were required to call out, "Unclean," so that everyone could move away from them and not be contaminated by their presence. What a sad existence! But Naaman's life was about to be turned around—if he could just find it within his heart to humble himself.

How amazing that a great and honorable man was moved by the words of "a little maid"!

Naaman's wife had a maid, a servant, who was a native of Israel. She was described in scripture simply as *"a little maid"* (Verse 2), but she was about to be used by God to change the life of this great and honorable man.

The maid told Naaman's wife that if Naaman could just get to God's prophet in Israel, he could be healed. She didn't have to say this, because she was just a servant, but God uses the humble, and she was led to say it, so she took the risk. The amazing thing is not that she said it, but that Naaman put stock in her words and actually set out to find the prophet she had mentioned. How amazing that a great and honorable man was moved by the words of *"a little maid"*! God is so great.

Naaman Needed Some Humbling

So Naaman came with his horses and with his chariot, and stood at the door of the house of Elisha.

2 Kings 5:9

Naaman arrived in Israel in his fine chariot, his personal Mercedes. He was, after all, a man of great wealth, and he therefore thought highly of himself. But when the man of God heard that this respected foreign dignitary had come, he quickly discerned something about Naaman that he didn't like. The man was not only infected in his flesh; he was infected in his spirit. He was proud, and pride is every bit as deadly as leprosy.

When Elisha sensed this about the man standing at his door, he decided not to even go to the door to greet him. Instead, he sent his servant to speak with Naaman. This seemed like a serious breach of protocol, but it had a purpose. God was trying to humble Naaman so that he could be healed.

And this process was indeed humbling. It was bad enough for a great man to be addressed by a mere servant, but the message the servant brought to Naaman from the man of God was not one that made Naaman very happy. The prophet said that Naaman should go and wash himself in the Jordan river, known to be at the time one of the nastiest rivers in the area. God was forcing this man into a very humbling situation.

When something like this happens to you, it has a purpose. So it's best to go through it so that you can come out as pure gold. If you don't, you'll just have to repeat the process. And that means it will take you longer to get to your next level.

But Naaman couldn't see any of that—at least not at first. He became angry because the man of God had not come out to greet him. At the very least, he could have waved his hands over him so that he could be healed. As it was, the man of God had done nothing—except suggest that Naaman go and wash in a muddy river.

God never does things the way we expect Him to. He said:

> *For my thoughts are not your thoughts, neither are your ways my ways, saith the* Lord. *For as the heavens are higher than the earth, so are my ways higher than your ways, and my thoughts than your thoughts.*
>
> Isaiah 55:8-9

God always knows what He's doing, and one of the things He knows is that the way up is always down. It is necessary to humble ourselves before we can be exalted. So always do things God's way, and you'll come out just fine.

SECOND-GUESSING THE PROPHET

Naaman knew of at least two rivers that were better

than the Jordan, so next, he began second-guessing the prophet of God. What a mistake that was! We can never dictate to our leaders; we are to follow them, not second-guess them.

We must say, in fairness to Naaman, that he was right about the two other rivers, but that had nothing to do with it. When God says to do things a certain way, then that's the way to do them, and humility demands that we do it His way without question. Naaman, instead, was so upset that he turned and walked away:

> *So he turned and went away in a rage.*   2 Kings 5:12

This was a critical moment. Naaman had come this far to be healed, but the sad truth is that he was walking away angry and still a leper. Would he miss his day of visitation? If we're not willing to do things God's way, then we cannot receive what we're believing Him for.

GOD USES ANOTHER SERVANT

Fortunately, one of Naaman's servants who had accompanied him on the journey had more sense than his master did at that moment. Again we see a humble person speaking wisdom to this great and honorable man. The servant gave a very soft and respectful answer, and, as the wise Solomon said:

> *A soft answer turneth away wrath: but grievous words stir up anger.*   Proverbs 15:1

This servant suggested to his master that he had nothing to lose by trying what the prophet was suggesting. The worst thing that could happen was that he would go home wet and muddy. This logic was so simple, and yet pride had prevented Naaman from seeing it himself. Pride, as we established early on, is blinding, and if you don't deal with it, it will cause you to miss what God has for you.

So it's always best to do things God's way—whether we understand the reasoning behind them or not. Naaman had to obey God and His servant if he was to receive his blessing. The man of God had told him to go to the Jordan and dip seven times in its waters, and that's exactly what he had to do—nothing more and nothing less.

WHAT WOULD HAVE HAPPENED?

What would have happened if Naaman had gone on home angry? Nothing. His leprosy would have gradually gotten worse, and his story would have ended sadly.

What would have happened if Naaman had gone to the Jordan and dipped, but only three times? Again, nothing! We have to follow God's instructions to the letter. When Naaman eventually humbled himself and followed all the instructions he had been given, he received his healing immediately:

He was clean.   2 Kings 5:14

It's difficult to imagine that moment. A few moments before this man had been a hopeless leper, and now he had a new lease on life. He must have been a very happy man in that moment, and he must have been very thankful to his servant for suffering his insolence and offering him kind words of wisdom. But he had nearly missed it because of his foolish pride and arrogance.

SOME MORE HUMBLING

Naaman was so grateful for this miracle that he turned back to bless the man of God. The Scriptures are clear that we should return a natural blessing when someone has given us a spiritual blessing, and the deeply rooted tradition of the Middle East would not allow Naaman to go home without making this gesture of gratitude. This time, however, it was not to be.

As a further means of humbling Naaman, so that he could retain his healing, God told Elisha not to receive anything at all from Naaman. This was not only a humbling experience for the foreign officer; it was also a humbling experience for the prophet.

> *The deeply rooted tradition of the Middle East would not allow Naaman to go home without making this gesture of gratitude!*

As Naaman went his way, he must have pondered all of this. Why would his gifts be refused? He still had a lot to learn.

A TRAGIC TURN OF EVENTS

The story might have ended with this, but then something terrible happened. Until that moment, everything had worked as the Lord willed. Naaman had been healed, he had offered his thanks, and he was now on his way home rejoicing. But this great military leader was not the only one struggling with pride. Gehazi, Elisha's servant, was having a struggle of his own.

He now decided that Elisha had been too easy on Naaman. If Elisha didn't want those lovely gifts, he could use them himself. Without consulting Elisha, he decided to go after Naaman and get the goods for himself and his family. He would have to lie to Naaman and say that Elisha had sent him to bring them back, and then, when he got back home, he would have to lie to Elisha about where he had been. This is the problem with pride. It leads to so many other evils. In this case, one of the evils involved was money, and money, or rather the love of money, also leads to many other evils:

For the love of money is the root of all evil: which while some coveted after, they have erred from the faith, and pierced themselves through with many sorrows.

1 Timothy 6:10

NAAMAN'S TURNAROUND

Everything that Gehazi did was foolish, but how utterly foolish it was of him to lie to Elisha! He had traveled with the man of God and knew all about his ministry. This was the man who had called fire down from Heaven upon his enemies and done many other great miracles. He seemed to know everything there was to know about everyone. How would he not know what his own servant had done?

Maybe Elisha didn't know everything, but at the very least, he knew everything God wanted him to know. In this case, he knew immediately that Gehazi was lying, and, although he loved and appreciated the servant, he was now compelled to speak judgment over him. He could not do otherwise.

GEHAZI'S END

The end result was that Gehazi received in himself the leprosy of which Naaman had been so gloriously healed. How sad!

In this remarkable story, one man (Naaman) chose to be humble and was blessed with a new lease on life, and another man (Gehazi) had to be humbled and was cursed. What must have been his end?

Never allow the devil to deceive you into becoming hard-hearted, self-willed and unthankful. Humble yourself under the mighty hand of God, and He will exalt you in due time. *Humble Is the Way!*

෯

CHAPTER 7

A WOMAN GETS WHAT SHE DOESN'T DESERVE

And, behold, a woman of Canaan came out of the same coasts, and cried unto him [Jesus], saying, Have mercy on me, O Lord, thou Son of David; my daughter is grievously vexed with a devil.   Matthew 15:22

When any person is humble, they move the hand of God. There are many Bible stories that illustrate this point, but one of them is so powerful that I must include it here.

A certain Canaanite woman heard about Jesus and what He was doing and decided to take her daughter and go to meet Him. What she met, at first, was nothing but frustration.

"HE ANSWERED HER NOT A WORD"

Because this woman was not a Jewess, Jesus, at first, didn't even answer her question. He had been sent, He said, to *"the lost sheep of the house of Israel."* His disciples agreed and tried to send the woman away:

But he answered her not a word. And his disciples came and besought him, saying, Send her away; for she crieth after us. But he answered and said, I am not sent but unto the lost sheep of the house of Israel.   Matthew 15:23-24

It must have been humiliating for this woman that she had made the effort to get to where Jesus was, but then, when she had cried out to Him for help, He hadn't even been willing to answer her. He could have said *something*, but He didn't say even one word. That would have been enough to infuriate most people and send them on their way. How dare this man treat her like that!

"Hey, Jesus, what's wrong with You?" most people would have shouted. "You're nothing but a racist snob! Hey, don't you hear me talking to You?"

But this woman was different. What Jesus did that day did not infuriate her or cause her to go off in a huff. She was determined to get help for her child, and she was ready to do whatever she had to do to get that help. Somehow she was convinced in her heart that Jesus had the answer she was seeking, so she stayed right there and continued to worship Him and ask for His help.

SHE WORSHIPPED HIM

Then came she and worshipped him, saying, Lord, help me.   Matthew 15:25

A WOMAN GETS WHAT SHE DOESN'T DESERVE

Many people sought Jesus' help, and no doubt not all of them were sincere. Some, we know, only sought Him for the loaves and the fishes, and others refused to turn back and give thanks when they were healed. What would this woman do? When she began to worship Him, she eventually got the Lord's attention.

Worship is humility! Worship recognizes who He is and who we are: He is the Creator, and we are mere creatures. Worship, therefore, pleases God. It touches His heart and moves His hand on behalf of the worshiper.

> *When the Canaanite woman began to worship Him, she quickly got the Lord's attention!*

SHE PRAYED, "HELP ME!"

As the woman worshiped, she prayed, "Lord, help me." That's a prayer of humility. It recognizes not only that He *can* help because of who He is, but also that we desperately need His help. We cannot do without Him. We should not let a day go by without asking the Lord to help us.

This prayer also personalized the woman's help. We are the ones needing God's help, and we must stop blaming our spouse or our children for our problems. "Help me, Lord." Continually blaming others for our woes is prideful and arrogant.

The Lord is waiting for your call: Help ME!

HE CALLED HER A "DOG"

Then, Jesus answered the woman, but what He said to her didn't seem to be very polite or very friendly. He actually called her a *"dog"*:

> *But he answered and said, It is not meet to take the children's bread, and to cast it to dogs.*
> Matthew 15:26

That response would have set most people off on an angry tirade, but not this woman. Today, many centuries later, we understand what Jesus was saying. His first duty was to the people of Israel. He had come into the world because He loved every man and was not willing that any should perish, but before He reached out to others, He must first reach His own. But surely this Canaanite woman could not have understood all of this at the moment. Still, she refused to be offended and, instead, answered the Lord's apparent insult with great wisdom and kindness:

> *Truth, Lord: yet the dogs eat of the crumbs which fall from their masters' table.* Matthew 15:27

A WOMAN GETS WHAT SHE DOESN'T DESERVE

Most people would have reacted violently if someone called them a dog. "How dare you!" I hear them saying. "Just who do You think You are? I don't care who You are! My husband may not be here to defend me, but I can defend myself!"

This woman had to be offended by His words. After all, what Jesus said is still jarring to us today, even after we understand the reasoning behind it. But she made a conscious decision to hold her peace and to try to understand what He was saying and why. As a result, her response was one of humility and receptiveness, and it moved the heart of Jesus.

JESUS WAS MOVED BY THIS RESPONSE

Then Jesus answered and said unto her, O woman, great is thy faith: be it unto thee even as thou wilt. And her daughter was made whole from that very hour.

Matthew 15:28

How wonderful! This woman, who, because she was a Canaanite, deserved nothing from the Lord, got what she didn't deserve.

When Jesus rewarded her, He spoke of her great *"faith,"* but He also might have spoken of her great humility. Faith works by humility, and when humility is absent, faith doesn't work.

Our Lord was so moved by this woman's attitude that He was willing to give her anything she asked for. Of course He knew her heart and knew exactly what she wanted. He said to her, *"Be it unto thee even as thou wilt."* And what had she wanted? Her child was desperately vexed by demons, and she wanted her to be delivered. Now: *"her daughter was made whole from that very hour."*

The timing of this miracle is notable: *"From that very hour."* Just as God's response to pride is immediate and decisive, His response to humility is also immediate and decisive.

Healing, at that particular time, had not yet been for the Canaanites. Jesus had been sent *"to the lost sheep of the house of Israel."* Still, in this case, He made an exception. Here was a woman of true humility. She sought Him. She worshiped Him. She refused to be offended by His words, and she obeyed Him. In the end, she got just what she wanted. What a powerful example she is to all of us! *Humble is the Way!*

CHAPTER 8

WHAT DOES ALL OF THIS MEAN TO US TODAY?

Now all these things happened unto them for ensamples: and they are written for our admonition, upon whom the ends of the world are come. Wherefore let him that thinketh he standeth take heed lest he fall. There hath no temptation taken you but such as is common to man: but God is faithful, who will not suffer you to be tempted above that ye are able; but will with the temptation also make a way to escape, that ye may be able to bear it.   1 Corinthians 10:11-13

Lucifer, Saul, Uzziah, Ananias and Sapphira, Naaman, a Canaanite woman ... what good does all of this do us if we don't know how to relate it to our own daily lives? But that's exactly the purpose of all Bible history, to teach us so that we don't repeat the same mistakes others have made. These were our *"ensamples,"* or examples, and we can learn from them.

It's interesting that the very next verse shows us that we're not alone in our temptations. Others have suffered

Pride is a killer, and we need to get rid of it as quickly as possible so as not to reap the punishment it inevitably brings!

or are even now suffering the same, so we can help each other overcome and be the people God intended us to be.

SOME GENERAL PRINCIPLES REGARDING HUMILITY

There are some general principles that we learn from these cases. The most important, of course, is that pride is a killer, and we need to get rid of it as quickly as possible so as not to reap the punishment it inevitably brings. God hates pride, He resists the proud, and I, for one, don't want to be caught among that cursed group.

Secondly, respect for God and submission to Him requires that we submit to the particular human authorities He has placed over us. Rebellion against authority is, in God's eyes, rebellion against Him. These two principles, if applied, will immediately and amazingly improve all our relationships.

God, instead of being our enemy, will suddenly become our Friend, and that will make all the difference in the world in our daily living. But, our newfound humility will also affect all of our other relationships—for the better.

In Part V of the book, I want to give you more specific teachings on how to improve all your most important relationships through humility, but first let me tell you about my own struggle for humility. *Humble Is the Way*!

PART III

MY OWN PERSONAL STRUGGLE FOR HUMILITY

CHAPTER 9

"NO ONE TELLS ME WHAT TO DO"

Let every soul be subject unto the higher powers. For there is no power but of God: the powers that be are ordained of God. Whosoever therefore resisteth the power, resisteth the ordinance of God: and they that resist shall receive to themselves damnation.

Romans 13:1-2

As I indicated in the Prologue, my struggle for humility began very early in life. Daddy died when I was just thirteen, and my Mom was left to raise our family. There were nine of us altogether, but my two older sisters were gone from the home. That still left seven of us sons at home. This was not an easy task, for Mom now also had to work to support us. We boys quickly became very independent and sometimes unruly.

My father had been hard on us, beating us every chance he got, seemingly for any reason at all—or no reason. I'm sure that sometimes I needed it, but there were other times when I didn't and got it anyway. He just seemed to be letting off steam. After he was gone, I developed a new motto for life, "No One Ever Tells Me What To Do," and I learned to fight to enforce it. Before long, I could beat boys and men much larger than myself, and I was always ready for a fight. This attitude set me at odds with anyone whom I interpreted as a threat to my independence. To avoid confrontations, I tried to be completely self-sufficient.

So, by the age of fourteen, I was on my own, having my own apartment and making my own decisions in life. I did what I wanted to do, when I wanted to do it and with whom I wanted to do it, and I was answerable to no one. That wasn't always possible, especially since I was still in school.

BEING EXPELLED FROM SCHOOL

My attitude got me into some serious trouble one day at school. I was feeling very hungry that day for two very different reasons. The night before, I had gone by Mom's house to give supper to my younger brothers. After all of them had eaten, I served up the last portion for myself. But before I could eat it, one of them complained that he was still hungry, so I gave it to him instead and went without. Also I was smoking pot, and that always made me very hungry. There was a long food line that day in the cafeteria, and I felt that I just had to have something to eat right that moment, so I jumped in front of some other students and then dared them to say anything to the teacher who was monitoring us. But they didn't have to say a word. The teacher saw me, and he came my way very quickly.

"You," he said, "get out of the line! I saw you! You don't cut in front of everybody else. Get to the back of the line!"

But that was not something I wanted to hear. Something came over me, and I told the teacher that if he didn't step away from me, I would knock him out. That was daring, because he was a big man, and I weighed only a little over a hundred pounds. But I meant it.

My attitude got me into some serious trouble one day at school!

"What did you say?" he demanded.

"You heard what I said," I insisted. I was ready to fight, and I probably would have if some of the other boys had not held me off.

This, of course, resulted in my being sent to the principle's office and being expelled from school for a week. I felt so dumb, sitting at home watching cartoons when all the other students were in school, but I just couldn't control my big mouth, and it was forever getting me into trouble. I didn't like submitting to people I felt threatened by.

That week I had a lot of time to think about my attitude. If I was going to finish school (and I desperately wanted to) something would have to change in me. When the time of my expulsion was over, I returned to school, but nothing much had changed. I was more polite on the outside, but inside I was still boiling.

My Stint in the US Marine Corps

I and two of my buddies thought of ourselves as being very tough, and when we heard that Marines were tough and that the Marine Corps actually paid you for being tough and taught you how to be more tough, we thought that was the place for us. So after high school, we enlisted.

What we hadn't counted on was the extreme submission we were taught to our superiors. There was a definite chain of command in the Corps, and anyone wanting to survive had better learn it quickly and submit to it willingly. Otherwise, life became unbearable.

In some ways, the Marines just made my problem worse. During my time there, the feelings of anger, frustration and rebelliousness inside of me only intensified. Now I learned not only how to fight, but also how to kill.

Paid Killer would have been a good job description for me about then. In my training, I was taught how to take people out. I could do it with a knife, I could do it with my rifle, and I could do it with my bare hands. And, what's worse, something in me caused me to enjoy every minute of it.

"NO ONE TELLS ME WHAT TO DO"

When my four years of enlistment were up, I felt that I was ready to get out of the Corps, but I was told by my superiors that they wanted to recommend me for Special Forces as a Recon Ranger. My ability to inflict physical harm on others was exceptional, they said. The Recon Rangers learned how to jump out of helicopters without parachutes and land in trees and survive. They learned more ways to maim and kill, and they mastered all the martial arts. That was very tempting to me because there was something in me that loved a fight, but in the end I decided that I wanted out from under the stress of constantly having to submit to authority. In the Marines, I had become a heavy drinker, a curser, and it was my time to enjoy the high life—free of all constraint or responsibility.

My Initial Surrender to God

My grandmother kept inviting me to go to church, but I told her I wasn't ready for that. I was having too much fun. I was out partying in the clubs and having what I thought was a wonderful time. But I can never forget what happened on two occasions.

Once, I was out on the dance floor slow-dancing with a girl, and I distinctly heard the Lord's voice, "I'm coming back in a time when you least expect it." This so startled me that I left her there and went to the bar to drink.

On another occasion, I was again dancing, but to a stronger beat. The red lights were flashing, the smoky mist was swirling, the music was throbbing, and I was out there shaking myself for the devil.

I had never thought about it that way before, but suddenly it came to me as clear as day that this was exactly what I was doing. Then, suddenly, I heard God speak to me. "What are you doing?" He asked.

Everywhere I was, it seemed, God's hand was upon my life, and He was calling me. He had known all along that He wanted to make a preacher out of me, and that night He opened my understanding enough to realize that I was out there shaking myself for the devil. Instead of submitting myself to God and resisting the devil, I was resisting God and submitting myself to the devil. How could I expect to be blessed?

> *"What am I doing here? I don't belong here!"*

"What am I doing here?" I asked myself. "I don't belong here. I was raised in church, and I should know better." And I couldn't take it anymore. Again, I left my girl there on the dance floor and went to the bar and ordered a double. I thought I could drown away all those thoughts that were troubling me, but I found that I couldn't do it. I couldn't party away the hand of God that was upon my life, and I couldn't get high enough to forget God's call. Every time I came down, there He was ... still dealing with me. I had to make things right with Him somehow.

How It Happened

My uncle was a preacher and often invited me to his church, but I always put him off. Church wasn't for me ... not yet anyway.

I had become an alcoholic, and one day I was lying stretched out in bed much as Jesus had been on the cross. Whether I was awake or asleep I've never been able to remember. What I do remember is that I suddenly saw a woman coming through the side of the wall by my bed. She had long black hair and was dressed in a long white robe. She was squatting like an Indian in mid air, hovering over my bed. "This is the way your Savior was stretched out for you," she said. "He died, so that you might live. You haven't been willing to listen to a man, but you will listen to a woman. At your weakest point, God will reach you." And, with that, she went back out through the wall. From that moment on, for some reason, my life seemed to fall apart, and I became desperate for a solution.

A Woman at a Train Station

Then one day a woman approached me at a train station. She was very polite, but also very insistent. She witnessed to me about Christ, and when I told her that I had grown up in church, she said, "You know you have a call of God upon your life, and you're not doing anything about it. It's time for you to make a decision to surrender your all to Him."

"If you died today, you'd go straight to Hell, and that's not what you want. Why not yield your stubborn will to God?"

I was able to put her off, but when I was alone, I cried and remembered the dream. Something had to change. I was very miserable.

INVITED TO A REVIVAL MEETING

Not long afterward at work one day, a co-worker told me they were having revival at his church and invited me to attend. "I couldn't," I told him. "I don't really have anything suitable to wear."

"That wouldn't matter at all," he assured me. "Nobody's going to care what you have on. We're having a very special evangelist, and I think you would enjoy him." So I went.

I sat at the back of the church, and as I listened to the preacher, I liked what he was saying, but I wondered if I could live the life that would be expected of me. Probably not, I concluded, and when the time came for people to respond to his call, I held back.

As I was leaving the church that night, the pastor met me at the door and spoke to me, thanking me for coming. "Always remember," he said, "this is the House of God, where everybody is somebody." I liked that, and I liked him. He didn't make me feel uncomfortable at all. In fact, he was very warm and easy to approach. "If only my own father had been like this," I was thinking, "my life might have turned out very different."

"Come back tomorrow night?" he invited, and I surprised myself by telling him that I would. That was Thursday, and so the next night was Friday. I had forgotten that it was my party night.

I Almost Lost My Life

The next day in the plant, my boss came by and handed me my paycheck, and my first thought was to get my pals together for a good party that night. Then I remembered my promise to the preacher to come back that night. Why had I ever promised to go to church on a Friday night? That was crazy. I had sometimes gone with my Mom on a Sunday, but go to church on Friday? Never! That was always my best party night.

As I went about my work I struggled for a while with the decision of whether to break my promise to the pastor or not. With all of my faults, I had always been a person of my word. If I said I was going to do something, I did it. But I had money in my pocket, and this was Friday. How could I go to church? Eventually, my flesh won the argument, and I decided to party hard that night.

Not long after making that decision, I slipped and fell onto the conveyor belt. Car parts crashed up against me, and people from every side began to converge to see what was happening.

As I struggled helplessly to get up, I began to hear an ominous sound. It was my own heart, beating wildly at first, but then slower and slower. I could hear every beat, and it seemed that my heart was failing. "Oh, God," I prayed, "don't let me die here. I'll go to church tonight. I'll keep my promise to Your house. I'll go hear Your Word."

The beats came slower and slower, and I could see the look of horror on the faces around me. Everything seemed to be in slow motion. "No, God," I prayed. "Don't let my life end like this. I humble myself before You. I will do Your will. Have mercy! Please have mercy!"

Then it seemed that my heart had actually stopped, and I was taking my last breath. But with that breath, I cried out once more. "Lord, I promise that I will go to church tonight and serve You. Don't let my life be ended prematurely." There was a torturous moment's pause, and then my heartbeats slowly came back to normal.

I WAS ALIVE

"Are you okay?" my worried co-workers asked. I was. I was alive and well and determined to do God's will.

That night, as I was getting ready for church, my friends came by to get me for the party. "I'm going to church," I told them.

"You're what? Don't be crazy!" they said. "It's Friday night."

"No, really," I insisted, "I'm going to church. You can't save me, and I need to be saved." They had no answer for that.

I went to church that night and got saved and filled with the Holy Ghost. At last, I had surrendered my life to the Almighty and taken the first steps in humility.

LEARNING TO TAKE MY FIRST STEPS IN HUMILITY

I was now saved, and I knew I was on my way to Heaven, but I didn't really know how to be a Christian. Because I had recently left the Marines, I was a fighter, a curser and a drinker. Now that I was saved, I would have to go to the house of God regularly to learn how to walk in this new way. I had a LOT to learn.

> *At last, I had surrendered my life to the Almighty and taken the first steps in humility!*

As little children, we all had to learn to walk physically, and as newborn children of God, we have to learn to walk spiritually in humility before God. It doesn't come automatically. I found that, although I had taken that initial step of yielding myself to God, there was still a lot of rebellion in me. God would have to help me know how to act from day to day in a way that pleased Him.

Some people have been Christians for many years, and still they haven't learned how to walk with God in humility. That's a tragedy that needs correcting. But at the moment, I was in the same boat.

Being a Christian meant that I had to submit to my pastor, and this was made easier by the fact that I genuinely liked this man. He quickly took me under his wing, spent time with me and taught me in every way he could. I sensed that he loved me and wanted the very best for me, and that made submitting to him almost a joy—almost. *Humble Is the Way!*

CHAPTER 10

LEARNING HUMILITY THROUGH DISCIPLINE

Verily I say unto you, Except ye be converted, and be-come as little children, ye shall not enter into the king-dom of heaven. Whosoever therefore shall humble him-self as this little child, the same is greatest in the king-dom of heaven. Matthew 18:3-4

Many of my early experiences with humility were learned through the church's policies of discipline and through God Himself imposing some discipline upon me or others. As I stayed in the church and observed the teachings, I began to see what true humility was all about in practical terms.

MY FIRST TASTE OF REBUKE

One day both the pastor and I needed to go to the restroom at the same time, and there was only one men's room, so while he was in there, I took the liberty of using the ladies' restroom. I saw nothing wrong with that, and I was therefore surprised when he began to rebuke me harshly for it. "No, Son," he said. "Never do that. You didn't think there was anyone inside, but there might have been, and that would have caused a problem. This is a church, and we have to think about these things."

Then, changing tones, he said, "Let's go get something to eat."

"That's all over now. Let's go get something to eat!"

I was startled. My pastor had just rebuked me rather harshly, and now he was inviting me to eat with him? I didn't understand and I asked him about it. "But, Pastor, you just rebuked me."

"Yes," he said pleasantly, "but that's all over now. Let's go get something to eat." And that's the way it was. He might rebuke me, but he loved me and wanted God's best for me. That was the way I was to learn, and I had to humble myself and receive it. I also learned from the experiences of others.

A Brother Is Disciplined

A brother in the church had been driving the church bus for a while, and our pastor was so impressed with his faithfulness that he decided to let him start ministering the Word. As often happens, this man quickly got puffed up and wanted to start telling the pastor what to do. The result was that not only was he *not* given further opportunity to preach; he was also removed from his post as bus driver.

The pastor's hope was that this discipline would turn the man's attitude around, but just the opposite happened. When he was disciplined, the man stormed out of the pastor's office offended. I was there to witness it, and the pastor turned to me and said, "Son, never do that to your leader. That's wrong. I promise you he won't be around here long." And sure enough, before much time had passed, that brother left the church.

After this man was removed from driving, the pastor himself began driving the bus, and I rode along with him so that I could learn more. He said to me one day, "Remember, Son, everyone is expendable in the ministry! Even me! God doesn't need you; you need God! Humble yourself before Him." I never forgot that. I was learning to walk humbly before the Lord—step by step.

I seemed to be doing well for a while, but then two things happened in close order that showed me that I had a long way to go toward true humility.

I "Lost It" with a Neighbor

From earliest childhood, we children had been taught to speak respectfully to our elders, and I usually did that. After I had become a young man, older people would sometimes curse me out, and I wouldn't answer them. This time, I wasn't as fortunate. I "lost it."

I was out one day walking my brother's dog Saint, when the dog ran after a cat and wandered into a neighbor's yard. I was a little alarmed when I noticed where Saint had gone because the owner of that property had a reputation for meanness in the whole neighborhood. "Come on, Saint," I called, but it was too late; here came the neighbor, and he was mad.

"You'd better get that dog out of my yard!" he shouted.

"Sorry, sir," I said. "I'll get him." And I called again, "Come on, Saint." But the dog didn't move fast enough for the man, and he had no patience with him.

"I'm warning you: Get your dog out of my yard right now," he insisted.

"Come on, Saint," I coaxed.

"If you don't get that dog out of my yard right now," he threatened, "I'll shoot him, and I'll shoot you too!" And he began to scream and curse, so that the neighbors heard it and quickly gathered around to see what was happening.

At that point, I'd had enough. This just seemed more than I should be willing to bear, and I turned on the man. "I tried to be nice to you, Old Man," I said (he wasn't all that old, but "Old Man" seemed like a proper salutation at the moment). "Now you've pushed me too far. You shouldn't have done that. If you had just accepted my apology and let me get my dog and go on my way, it would have been over. But you couldn't do that, could you? You had to curse me and embarrass me in front of everyone. Now, you got me mad, and I'm going to knock you out."

When I said that, all the neighbors around began to cheer. At last, someone had the nerve to tell this very offensive and confrontational man off. But I wasn't rejoicing. The fact that all my neighbors had heard my outburst brought me to reality. I knew that I was wrong. It had been my responsibility to watch the dog and keep him out of neighborhood yards, and I had failed. Then, provoked, I had said things I shouldn't have said. I walked away that day feeling like a failure.

Christian? What kind of Christian was I? I was just glad my pastor hadn't pulled up about then, for I surely didn't want him to hear what I was saying or see how I was acting.

ANOTHER SERIOUS INCIDENT

Then another serious incident happened, this one in church, and this time I couldn't hide it from my pastor.

I had been playing bongos since I was a boy, and soon after I was saved and joined the church, I was allowed to play with the church musical group. At other times, I was permitted to lead the worship, and I loved that too.

I had my own rather unorthodox style of playing the bongos, but people liked it, and I was proud of that fact. Then, one night in music rehearsal, one of the men of the group said to me, "You can't play those bongos right; let me show you how to do it," and he grabbed them and began to demonstrate his method.

That really got my dander up. "You play the bongos the way you want to play them," I told him, "but I'm going to play them the way I want to play them. And if you don't like it, then let's go outside and settle this like men." I meant it, and he could tell that I meant it.

He backed down immediately, with the words, "Well, it's not something I wanted to fight you over." But he must have gone directly to the pastor and reported the incident. Before long, I heard an ominous voice, saying, "Brother Jones, I want to see you in my office IMMEDI-ATELY!"

As I went down the hall toward the pastor's office, I felt like a little school boy again on his way to the principal's office. "Why, oh why, can't I just be more humble?" I asked myself on the way to the judgment hall. "Life would be so much simpler if I could just humble myself before others."

"Son," my pastor said, "is it true that you threatened one of the brothers in the musical group?"

I tried to answer, but all I could do was stammer, and this and my flushed appearance confirmed my guilt.

"Son," he said, "this is not good. You're going to have to be disciplined. You will sit down for a couple of weeks, and while you're sitting there, I want you to think about what you've done. You can praise God in your seat in the services, but I don't want you to play any musical instru-ments or to have any other part in the service or to be on the platform for any reason whatsoever. I want you to sit in the front row, and don't miss a single service."

Much of this was like a death sentence to me. I loved playing with the other musicians, I loved being up there with them and I loved it when I was given the opportunity to lead the worship service. Now I could do none of those things for the foreseeable future. And everyone would know why.

But he wasn't finished. "And," he concluded, "I don't want to ever hear of you threatening anyone again. You're not a Marine now; you're a child of God, and you're in the army of the Lord. So start acting like it."

IT SEEMED LIKE A HARSH SENTENCE

As he was delivering what seemed to me at the time like a very harsh sentence, I felt my blood pressure rising. It was the same feeling I'd had when the teacher told me to get out of line in school, the same feeling I'd had when the man cursed me for allowing the dog to wander into his yard, and the same feeling I'd had when the man criticized my method of playing the bongos. I didn't like to be told what to do, by anyone—even my pastor.

> *"While you're sitting there, I want you to think about what you've done!"*

I had a decision to make in that moment. Was it time to back down on my life's motto, "No one ever tells me what to do"? It seemed that I would have to—if I expected to stay in the church. They were very strong on submission, and I had long dreaded such a showdown.

What should I do? If I wanted to continue serving God, I had to submit to this man, and yet my flesh rebelled with all it was worth. Was I ready for a complete change of life-style? Was I ready to let someone else make a decision about my life? For a moment, my future hung in the balance, and what I decided could send me reeling back into the world or give me a chance to continue forward in God's Kingdom.

In the end, I decided that I really had no choice. It was either humble myself or lose out in the things of God. I now desperately wanted to submit myself wholly to Him, for I was tired of doing wrong and wanted to start doing what was right. And, since submitting myself to God meant submitting myself to those He placed over me, I had to do it. I knew that this man loved me and that what he was telling me was for my own good. I didn't like the idea of giving up control of my life, but what was the alternative?

His words hung in the air for a long moment, as I pondered my options. Then, at last, I managed to answer: "Yes, Pastor!" And I left his office that day a changed man.

SOME VERY DIFFICULT WEEKS

There was nothing easy about the next two weeks. I loved playing my bongos, and it was hard for me to just sit there and look at them as the other musicians played. The bongos seemed to call to me, but the pastor had said that I should do nothing but praise the Lord, so that was all I could do if I wanted God's best for the future. So, I just sat there and looked at the other musicians as they played during praise and worship.

I had no guarantee that this discipline would end after a couple of weeks. Pastor had left it rather open-ended. If he saw in me the desired change, then I could resume. If not, I had no idea just what the future held. I prayed seriously that God would receive my repentance and restore me to my position.

After two weeks had passed, Pastor came my way one day in service. "Son, I see that you have obeyed the Lord. Get up there now on the bongos again." And I joyously ran for the platform, quickly thanking the pastor and then thanking God in my heart that He had received my submission.

That short period of discipline did wonders for my soul. To be humbled in that very public way, being sat down for a period of time, had a sobering effect on me. I truly learned my lesson, and I never threatened anyone else again. It was, in fact, a life-changing experience. You can never beat humility. It's a great asset for anyone to have. I soon began to learn more and to grow more.

WHY PASTORS HAVE OVERSIGHT OF THE FLOCK

A certain man in our church kept telling the pastor

that he just had to have an opportunity to preach. Although a pastor is not required by God to let anyone else preach in his pulpit (and many pastors *don't* give anyone else an opportunity), thank God for those pastors who recognize that others need to grow and give them the opportunity to do so. Our pastor was like that. He knew when it was our time to preach, and he not only let us do it; he encouraged us to obey God.

> *"If I tell you that you're not ready, it means that you're not ready!"*

But there was a certain belligerence about this brother. He would get up in the pastor's face and insist that he was called by God and must be given an opportunity to preach. That was probably a good indication of what he was all about, and what happened to him as a result was pitiful, shameful and degrading.

One night, this man so vexed the spirit of the pastor that he said, "Okay, you can preach. Be ready for Friday night." He didn't think the man was ready, but he was tired of his posturing. The man was delighted and said that he would be ready.

That Friday night, when it came time for the preaching, the pastor got up and said, "Our brother tells me that he's called to preach. So, give him a great hand as he comes to preach to us tonight." It was noticeable that he had not said *the Lord* had told him that the brother was called to preach.

The brother got up and was very animated as he took the pulpit, but his enthusiasm soon turned to shame. When he tried to begin his sermon, he was suddenly dumbfounded and couldn't remember anything he had planned to say. He couldn't even get his text out.

After he had stammered for a while and it was obvious to everyone that he couldn't go on, the pastor started a song to rescue him. When the song was finished, Pastor got up and gave a little teaching on being ready. He said, "When I tell you that you're not ready, it's because I love you, and if I tell you that you're not ready, it means that you're not ready. God gave me the oversight of the church for a reason. You can say you're ready all you want to, but if you're not ready, then you're not ready. I want you to excel, so I will never willingly hold you back. Why would I do that?"

All this time, the humbled brother was sitting with his head hanging down, almost shell-shocked, wondering what had happened to him. He had forced his way to the pulpit because he was lifted up in pride, and God had humbled him publicly. That put the fear of God in the rest of us— me included.

About two years later, that same brother was preaching and preaching wonderfully. He *had* been called to preach; pride had just made him want to get started before his time, before he was ready.

SUBMITTING TO THE BISHOP

After four years under that pastor, my work took me to Atlanta, and I had to find another church and another pastor. This was when I found the bishop I spoke of in the prologue. He was a hard man, and it seemed difficult to submit myself to him. But through that full day of paralysis, God certainly got my attention.

I later asked the Lord why submission to someone I didn't consider to be very Christlike was so important. He reminded me of the case of Saul and David. What Saul was doing was definitely not good, but David insisted that he would not touch him because he was God's *"anointed."* What did that mean?

God showed me that it was not about the man. Because He had chosen to anoint this person, it was about Him. When we oppose a man or woman of God, therefore, we're not opposing a person; we're actually opposing God. That first lesson could have left me paralyzed for life, but God had been merciful. I didn't intend to let that happen ever again, but I would be tested of course.

TESTED ON MY RESOLVE

Not too long after that, the bishop asked me one day to help him hang some sheetrock in another church. Having experienced his sharp tongue and having suffered so much for my bad reaction to it, I was hesitant to accept. I did need the money, but I didn't need the hassles. Maybe I should pass this time.

When I hesitated, he said, "I'm going to ask you one more time: will you help me hang sheetrock or not?" I couldn't say no to the man, so although I dreaded being around him all day, I told him I would.

When we got ready to hang the sheetrock, he immediately began giving orders. "Now take the sheetrock and hold it like this while I cut it." I did what he suggested, but after a while, it got very tiring. I knew how to hang sheetrock, and it was not the way he was telling me to do it. Later, when he was occupied elsewhere, I began doing what I knew to do, and the work began to move faster.

He took note. "Boy, you're pretty good at that," he said, and it seemed for a moment that he was going to be nice to me. But that didn't last long.

"Come up on this scaffold," he demanded. "Come on, brother, we don't have all day; we have work to do." And he kept pushing me, as before, although I was working as hard and as fast as I could.

Eventually I felt that I couldn't take any more of his constant criticism and was about to say something unkind, but remembering what had happened the last time, I thought better of it. I didn't want to displease God in any way. So, instead of speaking out, I prayed and asked the Lord to help me show a humble spirit to this man.

"Watch what you're doing on that board," he shouted. "Stand up right." I just kept praying.

Then, suddenly the board on his side snapped, and he was falling. He was a big man, of some two hundred and fifty pounds, and I never understood what happened next.

Somehow I was able to balance on the beam on my side and catch him and pull him back up, so that he suffered only minor scrapes. There had to be angels helping me that day.

I was about to ask, "Bishop, are you okay?" when I heard the Lord say, "Just get back to work." So I did.

As I continued working that day, I heard the Lord whispering to me, "If you will hold your peace, I'll always fight for you." If we never see God move in this way, it's because we move Him out of the way and demand to handle things ourselves.

God is a gentleman. When we push Him aside, He yields and lets us do what we want to do. He will never force us. When this happens, we're on our own, and we're responsible for what happens next. (More on this important subject in Chapter 15).

DARING TO CONTRADICT MY PASTOR

I had to go back to Ohio for a while, and when I returned, it was to another part of the Atlanta area. Again, I needed to find another church and another pastor. This time, what I found was an apostle, and under his leadership I was to grow in leaps and bounds.

During my early years with the apostle, I still did a lot of menial jobs. I cut the church lawn, cleaned the toilets and drove the church bus. After many years of this, one day, without warning, a deacon of the church approached me and said, "Brother Jones, we have others who can do this work now. We appreciate you doing it, but your place now is by the apostle's side." And just like that, it was my time to move on up. I had paid the necessary price, and God was elevating me.

When it came to the question of humility, I was still far from perfect. One day I made the serious mistake of contradicting the pastor. There was no argument. I just told him that I didn't agree with something he had said, and he said that I was welcome to my opinion. That seemed to end the matter ... but God wouldn't let me off the hook so easily.

It was my habit to go into the woods to pray, and the next time I did that, God interrupted me in the middle of my prayer. I was praising Him and calling upon Him to bless me, and in the midst of all my noise, He broke through and said to me, "My servant knows. My servant sees. Now go back and humble yourself before him."

> *When we push God aside, He yields and lets us do what we want to do!*

There was something ominous about the way He said it, and I cried like a baby, afraid that judgment would fall upon me at any moment. I begged God not to let it happen before I had a chance to ask forgiveness from the pastor.

At the earliest opportunity I went to his office and knocked on his door. When I was invited in, I got on my knees before him and said, "Sir, you were right, and I was wrong. Please forgive me." Thankfully, he did.

We had a father/son relationship, and like many sons, I had gotten out of line and had to be humbled. It hurt, but I knew it would be good for me in the long run.

Just after that, I was asked to lead the praise and worship in the service, and when I got up, the Lord told me to confess my wrong and humble myself before the entire congregation. I tried to reason with the Lord, "This was just between me and him, God," but He wouldn't accept my reasoning. "There are some things in you that I have to work out," He said, and I knew that I had to do it—like it or not.

"Before I lead you in praise and worship tonight," I said to the whole congregation, "there's something I need to do." Then I turned to the man of God. "Apostle," I said, "you were right, and I was wrong. Will you forgive me?" I'd already done that same thing in private, but God wanted to seal it in public and further humble my spirit. The apostle graciously forgave me in front of everyone.

Learning to Submit Under a New Pastor

I stayed under that apostle for more than ten years, and then, when God sent me to the Houston area, again I had to find another pastor. This time, it was more important than ever because now I was a married man.

My wife and I met in Atlanta, but we were married and began our life together in Houston. We prayed together about who should be our pastor, for we loved the Lord and wanted to continue growing in Him, and we felt convinced that God led us in our choice of churches.

Still, I quickly learned that being under an apostle had been a very special experience, one that I had perhaps not treasured nearly enough. Now, I found, there was a very different level of anointing and a very different manifestation of the office of pastor in operation. This man I was under was just a pastor, and although we both had confirmation that we were in the right place, when he got up to teach us, I found it difficult to receive from him.

Somehow, I felt like I already knew everything this man was teaching, and I wanted something "more anointed." Nearly every service I went away disappointed. Then God showed me that pride was blocking my willingness to receive from this new and different pastor. I was sure I knew more than he did, and that was a recipe for trouble. I would have to get deliverance from that spirit of pride before I could go forward.

"Humble yourself," the Lord said, "or you'll never receive until you do." The moment I became obedient and humbled myself, I not only began to receive what the pastor was teaching; I got my own revelation from it.

"Wow, this man's taking us into the depths!" I said. In truth, he had been taking us into the depths all along, but

I just couldn't understand it because I was so lifted up in pride. I didn't have a tuned-in ear. I was sitting on the front row, and yet I couldn't see what the pastor was trying to show us. Isn't pride disgusting! No wonder God hates it so much!

When my eyes were opened in this way, I began praying for the man of God who was feeding us.

> *For the sake of our own soul, we can't allow ourselves to drift that way!*

GUARDING AGAINST DRIFT

One of the ways I humbled myself before God and the pastor was to be sure that I didn't fall into a daze and begin thinking of other things while he was preaching. That took some discipline, but I knew that if I did let myself fall into a daze, I would be missing out on what was being said. "Snap out of it," I would say to myself. "Something important is being said here, something you need to hear." I didn't want to be like so many—present in body, but absent in spirit and mind.

It's so easy to drift off into other thoughts and lose thirty minutes or more of an important teaching that's being given. If the pastor suddenly turned to some and said, "Tell me what I just said," they would be dumbfounded and unable to answer. For the sake of our own soul, we can't allow ourselves to drift that way.

AMENING THE PASTOR

Another thing I determined to do to humble myself and receive from the pastor's teaching was to urge him on with my comments. "Yes, Pastor," I said, as he preached. "Amen, brother." "That's it. Preach it. We need it." As I agreed with him, what he was saying registered in my spirit, and I was able to take it in.

My amening of the pastor had another effect, one I hadn't anticipated. There were some eight hundred people in the congregation at the time, and at the beginning, I was one of the few men urging the pastor on in this way. But as I was faithful to do it, others began getting behind the pastor, until the whole congregation seemed to wake up and begin to receive. My participation was suddenly blessing the entire congregation.

Many people have never learned how to work with a preacher. They don't know that their response feeds his anointing and allows him to go deeper. I began to realize that I was actually pulling the Word of God out of the man. He loved it, and I loved it too.

At the same time as I was encouraging the preacher and stirring the other members, I was receiving more myself. My perception of what was being said was deepening. "Come on, preacher," I would say, "you're in the Book now." And when he would start giving a scripture, I could actually finish it for him. I was with him, and I was helping him bring forth his message.

As I stayed in the Word and stayed before God, the Lord would often give me the message before the pastor had ministered it. His message then became a powerful confirmation to what God had been showing me. And that reinforced it in my spirit.

Of course, when I became a pastor myself, there were new levels of humility to learn. I'll deal more with that in Chapter 14, Humility and the Ministry. *Humble Is the Way!*

PART IV

HUMILITY AND
PERSONAL
RELATIONSHIPS

CHAPTER 11

HUMILITY AND MARRIAGE

Submitting yourselves one to another in the fear of God.
Ephesians 5:21

Yes, the Bible does command women to submit to their husbands. After all, someone has to take the final responsibility, and God has chosen the man. But although many men don't want to hear it, there is also a mutual submission that's necessary if marriage is to prosper and succeed these days. There was a time when women might stick by their man—even if he was physically abusive and never took her interests to heart—but that's no longer the case. Successful marriage in the twenty-first century demands humility and mutual respect.

SUBMITTING TO EACH OTHER

When we men are submitted to God, then we can also humble ourselves and submit to our wives, respecting their opinions and respecting their tastes. Every man must learn to love his wife, be gentle with her and give her the preferential treatment she deserves. "Yes, Baby, I understand," he might need to say. "I wanted to go out and get a steak tonight, but if you want shrimp instead, that's fine with me. We can have steak another time."

That's what it means to be a humble man in the little things of daily life. A man with that attitude is not always thinking of himself, and as a result, God will honor him. And his wife will love him too.

In my case, because my wife is Vietnamese, she loves Vietnamese food. I like it too, but not nearly as much as she does. That's only natural, because she was raised on Vietnamese food. For my part, I love pinto beans, mustard greens, corn bread, cabbage and fried chicken. Still, when she wants her style of food, I'm in agreement. If we can't be humble before one another, we'll never be blessed.

Sometimes my wife enjoys eating things I don't particularly care for (like octopus). Because she likes it, I prefer her and take her where we can find some octopus. That's what marriage is all about—being humble enough to meet each others' needs and desires.

God's Word is true, and when we learn His Word and obey His Word, it begins to have an impact on us personally. We're changed, and we're no longer selfish and mean to each other. Then failing marriages can be turned around. But the parties have to be willing to change.

LEARNING FROM ONE ANOTHER

Even though I've been saved longer than my wife,

and I know more scripture than she does, I've learned a lot from her. God has spoken to me and humbled me through her. Sometimes God speaks a word through her that simply "blows my mind." Sometimes I've said things to her and walked off, and then God has told me to go back and apologize because I don't know everything. Sometimes she's right, and I'm wrong.

This thing works both ways. It's never one-sided. God has commanded us to submit to each other, and that demands that we be humble. We can never approach the marriage relationship in pride. It simply won't work.

For instance, if you say that you're sorry for something, but you say it with the wrong attitude, it won't be well received. You need to get on your knees somewhere and wait until a change takes place in you. Then, you can approach your relationship with your spouse with very different results.

> *God's Word is true, and when we learn His Word and obey His Word, it begins to have an impact on us personally!*

"You were right, Sweetie, and I was wrong," is something we men need to say more often. I know it takes a lot for us to say these things because we never like to admit it when we're wrong. We're supposed to be right, after all, because we're the head of the household. But even the head makes mistakes, and we need to acknowledge that fact in humility.

What If She's the One Who's Wrong?

And what if your wife's the one who's wrong, and she refuses to humble herself and come to you with an apology? That's not your concern. You humble yourself because as the priest of the home, we men must set the example—whether the other party is humble or not. God has placed us as head of the family to lead by example, so that's what we have to do—regardless of what others do.

Friction in marriage is inevitable, as it is in all other relationships. This is more true in marriage because we make ourselves so vulnerable to each other. There's not a man and woman anywhere on the planet who can get along with each other a hundred percent of the time. But that's not a problem. The problem is when, because of pride, you refuse to be reconciled to each other, and you hold grudges, resent each other and lose respect for each other.

Be ready to admit it when you've been wrong. Did you speak out of turn? Did you misunderstand what was being said? Then confess that, and seek reconciliation. No matter what happens, keep loving each other and respecting each other, and you can work out any differences you might have.

WORK FOR PEACE

Men, we must stop getting angry at the drop of a hat. If you're not careful, you'll get yourself so strung out and bent out of shape that you'll have a heart attack. Stop trying to always have the last word. Stop insisting on speaking out, when you know very well that what you're about to say will cause all Hell to break loose. Just walk away and pray. God will help you find a solution.

Always remember that God's not the author of confusion. If there's confusion in your home, it means that someone is not walking in humility. The devil has snuck in a wedge between you. It may start with a simple look, but then come the smart remarks, and from there it escalates. Hurting one another, even with our words, is something we cannot afford to do. We're called to be peacemakers, not peace breakers.

I need peace in my home, just as you do, and all of us have to fight for that peace. Do whatever you have to do to keep the peace, and ask the Lord to help you. Jesus is the Prince of Peace, and He can bring peace to your troubled marriage.

YOU'RE THE PROBLEM

You must come to the point that you're sick and tired of *you*, not sick and tired of your spouse. Deliverance comes when you begin to see yourself as the problem. When you relate to people, any people anywhere in the world, there will always be some potential problem, something they do or say that will "tick you off," but God wants to deliver you from that. Your most important relationship outside of your relationship to Jesus, is with your spouse. Don't let it be a destructive one.

> **Don't be like the "silly women" mentioned in the Bible!**

Anytime you have a difference with your spouse, take it to a private place. Let your children go out for a few minutes to play. They don't need to hear their parents arguing. It will force them to take sides, and that's not healthy. This is between you and your spouse.

Never start screaming at each other in public. Keep it until the proper time and place, and then work it out in the proper attitude with humility on both sides of the issue.

WOMEN, DO YOUR PART

Women, do your part. Many women don't like it when we begin preaching God's Word that says that wives are to *"be in subjection to"* their husbands:

HUMILITY AND MARRIAGE

Likewise, ye wives, be in subjection to your own husbands.

1 Peter 3:1

Do you imagine that this *"subjection,"* or submission God is requiring is just in one area or in two or three things? Or is it to be in all things? Serving a husband is a privilege that God has given to the married woman, and she should accept it as such. Don't be like the *"silly women"* mentioned in the Bible: *"ever learning, and never able to come to the knowledge of the truth"* (2 Timothy 3:6-7).

Women, humble yourself and dedicate yourself to the welfare of your family. You're responsible, not only for the meals in your home, but to see that the Spirit of the Lord dwells there. And when you know what your husband loves and you're unwilling to give it to him, then you'll suffer the consequences. If he loves sausage and eggs for breakfast, fix them for him. Keep him satisfied, and he won't be looking elsewhere for his needs to be met. If you give your man what he needs, he'll stick by you in thick and thin.

Other women may come around with their suggestions about how your marriage should function. "Well, now, if I was you ...," they'll say. Just tell them they're not you, so you do what you know is right to do, and let others do what they want to do. He's not their husband, so you take care of him the way you know to take care of him, and don't be listening to the advice of every silly woman who comes along.

Every woman should know what her man likes, and she should know that it's her duty to give it to him.

MEN, DO YOUR PART

Of course, it works the other way too. Men are often worse about humbling themselves and doing the right thing than their wives. Paul wrote to husbands:

Husbands, love your wives, even as Christ also loved the church, and gave himself for it; that he might sanctify and cleanse it with the washing of water by the word, that he might present it to himself a glorious church, not having spot, or wrinkle, or any such thing; but that it should be holy and without blemish. So ought men to love their wives as their own bodies. He that loveth his wife loveth himself. For no man ever yet hated his own flesh; but nourisheth and cherisheth it, even as the Lord the church. Ephesians 5:25-29

What a high calling! Love her *"as Christ loved the church."* Some men boast, "When I tell her to jump, she asks 'How high?' " Oh, is that so? So you're the rooster in your hen house? Well, let me warn you. If you don't change your attitude, you just might get hit upside of your head with a skillet one of these days. That's not the way to treat the woman you love.

It takes humility to love a woman as she deserves to be loved, and you can't be guided by what other men are doing with their wives. The day you uttered that phrase, "I do," the two of you became one flesh and one spirit. So when you mistreat her, you're mistreating yourself. And if you try to get someone else's vision or someone else's desire and bring it into your home, you'll only cause trouble.

Outside influences will only bring disruption. Whatever she likes, that's what you're to give her—not what someone else suggests. Doing that will keep your marriage sweet and fresh.

GIVE HER WHAT SHE NEEDS AND WANTS

Some women love flowers and some don't. Sometimes what she needs is cash, not roses. Flowers quickly wilt and die. Give her something that lasts. What she wants is the most important gift you could give her. If she wants a new pair of shoes, and all you bring her is flowers, she'll be disappointed. Therefore, you have to know your spouse.

The Scriptures teach:

Likewise, ye husbands, dwell with them according to knowledge, giving honour unto the wife, as unto the weaker vessel, and as being heirs together of the grace of life; that your prayers be not hindered. 1 Peter 3:7

How are we to dwell with our wives? *"According to knowledge."* Do you have knowledge about your woman? If not, you'd better get some quickly or you'll have a hard time in life. You'd better humble yourself and learn what she likes and what she doesn't like, what she wants done and what she doesn't want done.

ALWAYS BE THE EXAMPLE

If a husband is not a good example, what can he expect from his wife and children? A man cannot rule his household by intimidation; he has to earn the respect of those over whom God has placed Him. He can't force his wife and children to love him and be kind to him, but if they know that he loves them and everything he does is for their welfare and future, they'll do it willingly and gratefully.

The problem with many men is that they consider humility to be contrary to manliness. Well, Jesus was a man, and He was *"meek and lowly in heart."* He never considered it to be below His manhood to serve others and prefer them. In your home, show that you're a real man, not by raising your voice or your fists, but by humbling yourself before others. People don't care how much you know; they want to see how much you care. *Humble Is the Way!*

Chapter 12

HUMILITY AND CHILD RAISING

Children, obey your parents in the Lord: for this is right. Honour thy father and mother; which is the first commandment with promise; that it may be well with thee, and thou mayest live long on the earth.

Ephesians 6:1-3

The many problems we are experiencing with our children these days have deep roots. In some measure, we may be able to blame the current culture of our country, the prevailing negative influences upon our children's daily lives and the failure of the public school systems to practice biblical principles. But there's a point where the blame game has to end. Our children are our children, and God is not holding other people responsible for raising them. We're their parents, so we're the ones responsible for teaching them God's ways.

GOD HOLDS US RESPONSIBLE

What can we expect from the world? What can we

*One
of
the
clearest
teachings
of
the
Bible
regarding
children
is
that
they
must
be
respectful
and
obedient
to
their
parents
at
all
times*

expect from child psychologists? What can we expect from public school officials? Fortunately, they're not our children's parents, and they're also not the ones who will stand before God and give an account; we are. The Bible has many clear and precise teachings for children (and for the parents of those children), and if we will teach our children what the Bible says and live it ourselves, we'll have fewer problems.

THE CLEAR TEACHINGS OF THE SCRIPTURES

One of the clearest teachings of the Bible regarding children is that they must be respectful and obedient to their parents at all times, but that requires humility, and we're not requiring humility of our children these days. Instead of growing up respectful and obedient, children are growing up self-willed and demanding, and that's a recipe for trouble. If children are not taught to respect their parents, then they also won't respect their teachers, and they also won't respect public officials. Walking humbly, including respect and obedience, always begins at home.

Many children today resent being told anything, and it's easy to see that they're headed for serious problems in life. God's Word declares:

Foolishness is bound in the heart of a child; but the rod of correction shall drive it far from him.
                                                        Proverbs 22:15

We simply cannot wait until a son or daughter becomes nineteen to begin disciplining them and demanding humility from them. By then, it's much too late. Now is the time, at whatever age they happen to be.

Far from being humble, respectful and obedient, many children these days actually rule the home. They tell their parents what they'll eat and what they won't eat. They tell their parents what they'll wear and what they won't wear. And they tell their parents what they'll do and what they won't do.

Children even go so far as to try to correct their parents, and that's way out of order. A parent who tolerates a child correcting or attempting to correct them is doing that child a serious disservice, and both will pay the price. If you do that, you're allowing them to practice disobedience and disrespect to your face, and that has consequences—for the both of you.

TEENAGERS OUT OF CONTROL

As a pastor, I counsel with many people who are encountering problems with their children these days. One day a lady called me. Her teenage children were being very disrespectful to her, and she was at her wit's end. She said she had tried everything, and nothing seemed to be working. I had to tell her that *she* was the one responsible for her dilemma. She had allowed her children to disrespect her when they were younger because their father was absent from the home. To make up for his absence, she had spoiled them, giving them whatever they wanted, and now she was paying the price. It was as simple as that.

Now they were too big to whip, but she had to do something because they were out of control. "What can I do?" she asked me in desperation.

I knew most she wasn't going to like what I was about to tell her, but I had to do it anyway. "If they're not willing to humble themselves before you, and they keep talking back, then your only option is to put them out of the home!" I told her frankly. "What they need is some tough love."

THE CASE OF MY BROTHER DARYL

I knew what I was talking about because I had experienced it myself. Once, when I was paying a visit to my mother in Ohio, she confided in me, "You have to do something about your brother Daryl. He won't listen to me, he gets into fights at school, he comes home any time he wants, he won't take out the trash or keep his room clean, and he's started sassing me. You're the oldest, and so you need to take care of it."

I knew that my mother was partly to blame for this predicament. Because Daryl was the baby of the family, she had spoiled him. As young as I was when my father died, it had fallen to me to discipline my younger brothers. Even when I was living on my own, I went by the house most every day to check on them and my grandmother who kept them. So disciplining Daryl was nothing new, but what could be done now? He was no longer a boy; he was now seventeen, and he was going to do what he wanted to do. It was just too late.

I tried to reason in this way with Mother, but she wouldn't hear of it. "No," she insisted, "you're the oldest, and you have to take care of this."

I prayed about what to do. I didn't want to have any hard feelings with my baby brother, so I asked God to give me wisdom.

When Daryl came home that day, I told him I wanted to talk to him, and he immediately became defensive. I could see that this was going to be difficult.

"Daryl," I began, "Mama says that you're not obeying her. You won't clean up after yourself, you come home late, and you're sassing her."

"Nobody's going to whip me again," Daryl quickly interjected.

"Did I say anything about whipping you?" I asked.

"I'm just telling you that nobody's going to whip me again," he repeated.

"Okay, Daryl, no one's going to whip you," I said, but then I suddenly grew very stern and raised my voice. "You may be too big for whippings, but if you want to act this way, then you need to get out of Mama's house. So get your clothes together and find another place to stay. You can't be disrespecting your Mama this way. It's not right. That's all there is to it!"

He was stunned by this response, for he'd never seen me like that before. "Well, where would I go?" he asked.

"You should have thought about that before you started acting so disrespectful," I answered, and I stood firm on my position.

THE DESIRED CHANGE CAME

Daryl went upstairs for about five minutes, and then he came down again, but he came down a very changed young man. All the bluster and defensiveness was gone, and he was his humble usual self again. In fact, he was crying.

"I'm sorry," he said. "I don't know what got into me. I know I need to respect Mama, and I won't disrespect her again. I promise."

"This is serious," I said. "You can't be disrespecting her again. No more sassing and you'd better do what she asks you to do."

"I will," he answered meekly.

When Mama came home that day, Daryl's room had been cleaned, all the trash had been taken out, the dishes were washed and Daryl was there to greet her.

"What did you do to Daryl?" she asked me when we were alone.

"I told him he had to get out," I answered.

"You did what?" she asked.

"There was no other solution," I told her. "He wasn't respecting you, so it was time for him to find his own place."

"But he's my baby," she protested.

"Mama, didn't you ask me to talk to him?" I said.

"I did," she agreed, "but I never imagined you would tell him to get out."

> *All the bluster and defensiveness was gone, and he was his humble usual self again!*

"Well, you got the results you wanted," I insisted. "So thank God that Daryl has changed."

She loved Daryl so much that it was difficult for her to imagine that putting him out could be a solution, but she never had those problems with Daryl again. And this was not an isolated case. I've found this to be a very effective way of dealing with rebellious teenagers. They don't know how good they have it, and when their support is suddenly cut out from under them, it has a very humbling effect.

Don't Dig Your Child an Early Grave

The Word of God teaches us that if children obey their father and mother, their days can be prolonged upon the earth, and that's a wonderful promise. But the reverse of that promise is also true. If a child does *not* learn to honor and obey his or her parents, they're in danger of having their life cut short.

Parents need to remind themselves that they're the parent, the responsible party, and that they're not helping their children by spoiling them or permitting them to be disrespectful. In fact, they're sending those children to an early grave by allowing them to act that way. If you're going to treat them that way, you might as well go out and dig their grave for them.

Many are sure that can't be true, but they need to read and then heed the Word of God. The wise Solomon wrote:

Be not over much wicked, neither be thou foolish: why shouldest thou die before thy time?   Ecclesiastes 7:17

Any of us can bring on his or her own premature death by foolish living, and when parents allow a child to live rebelliously, they're just facilitating that child's early demise. That's straight talk, but it's what we need to hear.

HUMILITY AND CHILD RAISING

God, in His infinite wisdom, has placed parents in the ladder of authority, under Himself, but over their children. And when children disrespect their parents, they're slapping God in the face and cursing Him, and He cannot permit that. Those actions, He assures us, will cause them to experience an early death.

GOD KNOWS WHAT CHILDREN NEED

God knows what you children need, and He said:

Wherewithal shall a young man cleanse his way? by taking heed thereto according to thy word.

Psalm 119:9

Your child cannot change unless and until they begin to take heed, and something has to bring their attention to the problem and the solution. Otherwise, they'll go on their merry way, doing whatever they want to do—regardless of who gets hurt. When children are out of control, parents must take difficult measures.

"But is it ever right to send your own children away?" some might ask. Well, when their stomach starts growling, they'll come back, and they'll have a different attitude when they do. When they remember the nice bed they had at home, they'll be back, and this time they'll be more respectful.

"And what if they don't come back?" Then that's not your problem. You've done what you could do, and the rest is up to them. In the meantime, your life will be a lot less stressful. Far too many parents live under terrible stress these days—all because of rebellious children.

REMOVING WITCHCRAFT FROM YOUR HOME

> *Rebellion is a terrible sin, likened in the Scriptures to witchcraft!*

Rebellion is a terrible sin, likened in the Scriptures to witchcraft:

For rebellion is as the sin of witchcraft, and stubbornness is as iniquity and idolatry.
1 Samuel 15:23

If rebellion appears, it must be broken off of young lives quickly and decisively, or they are headed for serious problems down the road. Knowing that rebellion will eventually kill should spur every parent to immediate action.

Do you have witchcraft in your home today? If so, it's a serious matter, and you must do something about it.

"But is it really a loving act to discipline your children?" many still ask. It's easy to see that those who ask such questions have been influenced by the liberal views of the "child-raising experts" of our day. God has made this point clear for anyone wanting to know:

HUMILITY AND CHILD RAISING

For whom the Lord loveth he chasteneth, and scourgeth every son whom he receiveth.   Hebrews 12:6

The Lord chastens those He loves, and you must do the same. Some parents still insist that their lack of discipline is because they love their children "so much." But that can't be right. If you loved them, you would be concerned about their future, and you wouldn't want them to die prematurely. If you loved your children, you'd do whatever is necessary to correct their behavior—just as God does with those He loves.

If you'll humble yourself before God, He'll show you how to rescue your children from trouble, and if they'll humble themselves before God and you, they will be saved.

LOOK FOR EARLY SIGNS OF REBELLION

Because rebellious children can bring us such heartbreak in life, we must begin to look for signs of rebellion early in life and nip them in the bud before they have a chance to grow. Scowling looks, if left unanswered, turn into scowling words. And scowling words, if left unanswered, turn into scowling deeds.

It's important for us to observe the countenance of our children. Watch their faces and don't let them get away with wrong looks. Conquer those looks now before they become something much more serious.

Ask a child, "Are you frowning at me?" If they are,

catch them now and correct them while you still have time.

A child's look is often an early form of rebellion. If you let that child get by with those early forms of rebellion, you're just setting the stage for more trouble down the road. That rebellion will grow until, at a certain age, you will no longer be able to handle that child. I know what I'm talking about. It happens again and again in our society and around the world. Stop it while you can.

Good parenting requires humility, and being a good and faithful child requires the same. *Humble Is the Way!*

∽

CHAPTER 13

HUMILITY AND THE LOCAL CHURCH

Obey them that have the rule over you, and submit yourselves: for they watch for your souls, as they that must give account, that they may do it with joy, and not with grief: for that is unprofitable for you.

Hebrews 13:17

To serve the needs of His little ones around the world, God has organized His Church into small units, or families, that we know as local churches. Within each of these local churches, He places mature people who are able to serve the others, just like parents in a home. We call these leaders pastors, because, like good shepherds, they care for the needs of the whole flock.

THE HUGE WORK OF PASTORS

The work of pastors, or shepherds, is huge. Those who are parents know what a large responsibility it is to govern one home, and that should give them an idea of just how difficult it is for a pastor to care for so many sheep at one time. All of the sheep are at different levels of spiritual maturity, all with different personalities and needs, and each one has a peculiar background that makes his or her case totally unique in many ways. The task of pastoring them seems literally impossible, and only the grace of God can make it work at all.

If the local church is to function properly, there must be a definition of who's who. The pastor must be the pastor, and the members must be the members. It would not do to allow a three-year-old to plan the menus for the entire family, and many so-called Christians are incapable of knowing what others really need. Even the best of Christians need time to grow and mature, so they must be children for a time, and someone must rule over them.

Knowing this, the writer of the Hebrews declared: *"Obey them that have the rule over you, and submit yourselves: for they watch for your souls, as they that must give account, that they may do it with joy, and not with grief: for that is unprofitable for you."* Obedience requires humility and submission requires humility, and these are not things any of us like to think about. And yet, the writer assures us, it's all *"for you."* So if you make life hard for the person God has placed over you, then you're just hurting yourself. They've been placed there to serve your interests.

THE MANY THINGS A SHEPHERD DOES

There are many things a shepherd does for the sheep, but one of the most important is feeding. Just as natural sheep need to be fed, we need to receive instruction from the Lord. And that's a problem for many people. They have to receive instruction in the home, in the school and in the work place, and they don't want more instruction when they get to church. But if there is no spiritual instruction, how are we to know God's ways, and how are we to grow in His ways? For the Christian, it is God's ways that should determine our conduct in the home everywhere we are.

The pastor must be the pastor, and the members must be the members!

So it's good when we can receive instruction, and it's even better when we can receive instruction in the right way, that is, with the right attitude. If you want to be wise, always welcome instruction in the things of God, for refusing to do so is an indication that you actually despise your own soul:

He that refuseth instruction despiseth his own soul: but he that heareth reproof getteth understanding. The fear of the LORD is the instruction of wisdom; and before honour is humility. Proverbs 15:32-33

If you can no longer receive instruction, then you're not humble. If you can no longer receive correction, then you're not humble. That's all part of walking with God and taking part in the daily life of the local church.

If you're like some, you may go to church and enjoy the singing, but when the preacher opens the Book to teach, all your joy suddenly leaves. Why's that? It's because he's going to start talking about you and where you're living. The Word of God always seems to have your name on it, and the preacher seems to be directing his comments specifically at you.

If you're wise, you'll welcome everything he says, and you'll pray to God and ask Him to help you to grow by it.

SUBMITTING TO GOD = SUBMITTING TO PASTORS

As we've seen, submitting yourself to God means submitting yourself to those in authority over your life. Then you can resist the devil, and he will flee. But he flees only when you are first submitted to God and then to God's order in your life. Therefore, a person who is submitted to God is also submitted to his or her pastor. If you can't submit yourself at home, if you can't submit yourself to your spouse, then you'll probably also find it difficult to submit yourself to a spiritual leader, and that is deadly.

I knew a woman once who got so angry with her pastor that she openly opposed him. That's scary, because, as we've now seen over and over again, when you oppose God's men, you're actually opposing God Himself. I prayed for that woman that judgment would not come to her, but she just got angrier and more belligerent.

Tragically, her son, who was a taxi driver, was shot and killed on his job one day. The passenger didn't even rob him, just left him for dead. We all hoped that this would mean a turnaround for the mother, but instead, she became even more angry and more critical. Before long, we were conducting that woman's funeral, and she had been in the prime of her life. She was visiting her brother, who was a pastor in Florida, and the both of them were found dead at the altar of his church, overcome by carbon monoxide fumes. I hope she was at that altar repenting, but who can know? Cases like that ought to make all of us think.

I knew the case of yet another woman who shook her finger in her pastor's face and told him she hated him and what he preached. The very next week, she died, eaten up with cancer. This is serious business, people, and we need a return of the fear of God among us.

CHOOSING LIFE OR DEATH

As with the obedience of children to parents, there is an element of life and death in our decision of whether or not to submit to a local pastor. We know what God's will is. He said:

With long life will I satisfy him, and show him my salvation.   Psalm 91:16

> **Many church members think that their role in the congregation is to constantly criticize and oppose the pastor!**

God wants to give you *"long life,"* but Satan's will for you is just the opposite. He wants to kill you, to cut your life short, to cut you down in your prime, and rebellion opens the door to him. Humility assures you a *"long life,"* but rebellion guarantees your early demise.

If you have hardened your heart against truth, God doesn't guarantee that His Spirit will always strive with you:

My spirit shall not always strive with man.
                              Genesis 6:3

Life or death? What's your choice?

Many die before their time, and no one seems to know why. Young men drop like flies, and there seems to be no explanation. Because it's your soul that's in the balance, don't be a fool and die before your time. God's Word warns us:

HUMILITY AND THE LOCAL CHURCH

The LORD shall cut off all flattering lips, and the tongue that speaketh proud things: who have said, With our tongue will we prevail; our lips are our own: who is lord over us?   Psalm 12:3-4

It's easy to see the pride in that statement, and it should be clear what the results will be. Always remember, the thief comes to steal, kill and destroy, but Jesus came to give us life and life more abundantly (see John 10:10). Submit to God's will (and His servants) and live.

REMEMBERING NATHAN'S REPROACH

There is one more aspect of local church life that I must address in this book. Just as children too often try to correct their parents, many church members think that their role in the congregation is to constantly criticize and oppose the pastor. That's a dangerous position to take.

Think about it: as wrong as David's sins were, none of his associates reproached him—not Abner and not any of the rest of his mighty men. Not one of them said, "David, that was wrong; you shouldn't have done that." Why? These men understood the chain of command. David was God's appointed king and their commander in chief, so it wasn't their place to be judging or reproaching him. God would do that in His own way. And He did; He sent Nathan the prophet to reproach the king and show him that he had done wrong.

Nathan told David a story of a rich man who had many sheep, and yet he stole the only lamb of a poor man. This particular lamb had not been raised for food, but as a pet, so it was beloved by its owner, and his loss was incalculable. The story was so moving that it got David's attention, and he asked who the man was and vowed to have him properly punished.

"You are the man," Nathan replied.

God has a way of getting our attention. He has prophets and prophetesses He can send to do the job, but one of the flock cannot take upon themselves this responsibility of correcting the pastor.

God is able to send someone to correct parents about the way they raise their children, and He's able to send someone to correct our bosses and our political leaders, as well. Leaving this responsibility with those God chooses assures that we will live.

To many, it just seems the right thing to do to be critical. They feel that they're somehow serving as checks and balances. But God didn't place that particular system in the Church. Those who believe this should read the Proverbs of Solomon:

There is a way which seemeth right unto a man, but the end thereof are the ways of death.

Proverbs 14:12

Some people who have attended our church told me that they were accustomed to speaking up to their pastor and correcting him. I let them know that they couldn't do this in our church. Maybe they got by with it out of ignorance before, but no more. They may have been perfectly right in what they were saying, but they were wrong in saying it, because that was not their place. Drop your critical spirit and come to church to learn.

SAUL BLAMED "THE PEOPLE"

When Samuel called Saul's attention to the presence of animals that were supposed to have been destroyed, he said they had been saved because *"the people"* wanted them to use in sacrifice. But when it comes to leadership, there are no excuses. Leaders are placed by God among us to lead, and they can't blame their followers for any failures that come as a result.

I've never yet seen a sheep with a staff in his hand, trying to herd shepherds, but we have them in the church today. May God help us because it's simply out of order, and He won't bless it. Sheep don't know how to lead shepherds, and they never will. Shepherds are called to lead sheep—not the other way around. It's the sheep that have to humble themselves to follow the shepherd.

Salvation, healing and deliverance come to us when we get our house in order and do things God's way. You can't expect to have miracles when you're disobeying God's prophets and rebelling against His express will. *Humble Is the Way!*

CHAPTER 14

HUMILITY AND THE MINISTRY

For I say, through the grace given unto me, to every man that is among you, not to think of himself more highly than he ought to think; but to think soberly, according as God hath dealt to every man the measure of faith.   Romans 12:3

Always, when we ministers preach, we're preaching to ourselves, as well as to others, and this is no more true than when I'm preaching about humility. But I also have to say that we can never preach what we have not first experienced. Therefore, when I write about the need for humility, I know what I'm talking about. I've lived it. Getting to where I am today has required a dying to the flesh, and it still requires a daily dying to the flesh to keep me in that place.

SOURCES OF PRIDE FOR THOSE IN MINISTRY

Just as pride has historically been a problem for those in leadership in the secular world, it has also been for those in leadership within the Church. We've had to overcome pride to get to where we are, and we have to battle it every day to stay where we are or to rise higher. There are many things that tend to tempt us preachers to *"think of [ourselves] more highly than [we] ought."* Here are just a few of them:

> *God has demonstrated His love to us in a very special way!*

- We did not get to where we are today without God's specific intervention on our part. He has demonstrated His love to us in a very special way.
- We started far down on the ladder, and the fact that we now find ourselves on higher rungs often causes us to forget just how far we have come or exactly how we got there.
- Being in ministry requires specific gifts and, along the way, God has graciously gifted us.
- We regularly experience the praise of people (as well as the criticism of others), and praise is always a danger to our souls.
- Usually, any promotion in God's Kingdom also involves financial promotion, and some are unable to handle this aspect of success.
- Being in ministry requires us to give orders to

others, and that sometimes makes us feel overly important.

JESUS' ANSWER TO PRIDE IN HIS DISCIPLES

Even the very disciples of Jesus had to fight the temptation toward pride. They argued among themselves about who was the greatest in the Kingdom, and Jesus had an amazing answer for them:

At the same time came the disciples unto Jesus, saying, Who is the greatest in the kingdom of heaven? And Jesus called a little child unto him, and set him in the midst of them, and said, Verily I say unto you, Except ye be converted, and become as little children, ye shall not enter into the kingdom of heaven. Whosoever therefore shall humble himself as this little child, the same is greatest in the kingdom of heaven.

Matthew 18:1-4

I'm not sure what these men were expecting to hear, but I am sure they were not expecting to hear that a little child was the greatest in the Kingdom. What did Jesus mean by this? What's great about a child, who is still largely untrained and unproven and almost certainly has little in the way of achievement to point to in life?

First of all, children have a pure heart. They have not yet been corrupted by the world. And we desperately need to return to that simplicity of spirit.

Second, a child doesn't try to hide anything. They just say what's in their heart. They call things the way they see them. And we desperately need to return to that simplicity of spirit.

But the most important point, the one that answers the original question of who is the greatest in the Kingdom is this: *"Whosoever therefore shall humble himself as this little child, the same is greatest in the kingdom of heaven."* Little children are still humble, and we need to return to that simplicity of spirit.

What does this mean? It means that no matter how God blesses you, stay humble. No matter what you accomplish in life, resist pride. The more you can stay humble, the more God can exalt you and increase you. As more and more ministry gifts and power come your way, it can be a danger to your soul. Stay humble, and nothing will move you.

Jesus said we had to become like little children if we were to enter the Kingdom of God, and He was very serious about it. This is no bluff. It's change or else. And this process of being converted and becoming as little children must be repeated over and over again. Every day brings a new challenge to the flesh, and every day we must die to self and be reborn in the Spirit.

DON'T INSIST ON ALWAYS BEING SEEN

One of the areas in which preachers are particularly susceptible to pride is that they're often tempted to want to be seen. Because of this, they always love to get right up front in every public function. This is not necessarily wrong, but if the motivation is wrong, then the act is dangerous.

Jesus gave a very specific teaching on this subject:

When thou art bidden of any man to a wedding, sit not down in the highest room; lest a more honourable man than thou be bidden of him; and he that bade thee and him come and say to thee, Give this man place; and thou begin with shame to take the lowest room. But when thou art bidden, go and sit down in the lowest room; that when he that bade thee cometh, he may say unto thee, Friend, go up higher: then shalt thou have worship in the presence of them that sit at meat with thee. For whosoever exalteth himself shall be abased; and he that humbleth himself shall be exalted. Luke 14:8-11

It's a rather funny scene to picture someone being moved down, but, in reality, there's nothing funny about it. We don't always have to be up front, and we don't always have to be seen. It's better to be asked up, rather than to be asked down. What this means is simple: walk in humility, and God will raise you up. I've seen it work time and time again.

Once, when I attended a service in Florida where R.W. Schambach was the speaker, I arrived early, hoping to get a good seat. As it turned out, the place was already packed, and I ended up in the very back. I wasn't very happy about being so far from the platform and the preacher, but I told myself to appreciate the fact that I was even present in the service.

Then, before long, an usher came and asked me if I would like to move up to the front row. There were two empty seats there, he said. I was delighted. I hadn't tried to push my way to the front, simply because I was a minister, but God, seeing my heart, had given me a seat up front anyway. And, on top of that, that night I ended up appearing on television and giving my testimony.

That testimony caught the attention of Brother Schambach, and he invited me and my wife to attend a special meeting he was conducting in San Antonio, Texas. We went, and the exact same thing happened in that meeting. The place was full, and the only seats we could find were at the back. We gladly accepted those seats, but then an usher came along and said, "Brother Schambach would like for you and your wife to move up front." It will work every time. Let God move you up, and don't force men to move you down.

ALWAYS REMEMBER THE PURPOSE OF MINISTRY

Many of our temptations to pride in ministry can be overcome just by reminding ourselves of what ministry is all about. Ministries have a purpose, and if we can understand that purpose it can guide our attitudes. Too many ministers somehow believe that the church was established for their employment, for their provision and for their convenience. But nothing could be further from the truth. You were established for the Church, not the other way around:

> *And God hath set some in the church, first apostles, secondarily prophets, thirdly teachers, after that miracles, then gifts of healings, helps, governments, diversities of tongues.*
>
> 1 Corinthians 12:28

Let God move you up, and don't force men to move you down!

God always has a purpose when He sets ministries and ministry gifts in the Church, and that's why He's requiring something of every apostle, prophet, pastor and teacher. They have a responsibility, and that responsibility is not to draw a paycheck; it's to perfect His people. There must be no other motivation in us, or we are in error.

We all need to be perfected, we're perfected by the Word of God, and that's why God has set ministers of the Word in His Church. All of these offices were set in the church for the perfecting of the saints. Bow before God and fulfill your God-given purpose in the Church, and you'll be a lot less likely to become proud.

Always Remain Teachable

There are many ministries among God's people that cannot yet come forth because those who are called have not yet humbled themselves. We all want to instruct others, but first we need to receive instruction ourselves. We cannot give out what we have not yet received, and we cannot lead others into things we have not yet experienced ourselves.

Wisdom begins with having a healthy fear of the Lord, and anyone who does not fear God, meaning that they have a healthy respect for Him and for His Word, is not fit for the Kingdom—let alone for the ministry. Then, once that fear of God is in place, it needs to be nourished with strong teachings from His Word. A person who hopes to do ministry must be teachable and must develop a solid and never-ceasing habit of learning.

Think of real life. Could you teach a child to tie their shoes if you had never learned to tie your own? How much more important learning is in the Kingdom of God! Always remain teachable, so that you can then teach others.

Learn to Wait for Your Promotion

Your promotion may not always come in the time you want it or expect it. That's God's prerogative. He has promised to exalt you, but He will do it in His own time.

What, then, can you do in the meantime? Know that

there is a set time for you to be lifted up, and then be faithful until that time comes. Whatever happens in the meantime, keep your spirit clean, keep your attitude right, and be ready. You don't know when your time will come. When it finally does come, will you be ready?

As you wait, you may see God blessing others. Never be offended by this. Your time is coming. God has a precise moment planned to set you on high. He has a definite moment to bring your promise to pass. Humble yourself and wait on His timing, knowing that it is perfect. The psalmist declared:

> *Wait on the LORD: be of good courage, and he shall strengthen thine heart: wait, I say, on the LORD.*
>
> Psalm 27:14

It took me until the age of forty to start my own crusades. Until then, I was helping other ministers and building other churches. I was undergirding other men and women of God and helping them bring their vision to pass. Then, suddenly it was my time.

Don't worry about your age, for age is just a number. God can use us at any age. Moses was eighty when he finally took up his torch of leadership. Until then, nothing had seemed to go right for him, but then suddenly he was able to deliver the children of Israel out of the hands of the Pharaoh. It happened because it was now his time.

God knew what He was doing all those years of my life. He always had in mind my reaching out to multitudes in the nations of the world, but I had a lot of getting ready to do. He had a lot of work to do in me, and it was only when that work had been accomplished that I would be ready to do His bidding. There's a set time in which you're to be brought forward, and it will only happen as you're able to humbly wait and prepare.

> *When your moment of promotion does come, be on guard against pride!*

ALWAYS BE ON GUARD AGAINST PRIDE

When your moment of promotion does come, be on guard against pride. A gift from God can be a wonderful thing, but if it brings pride to your life, it will also bring a curse upon you. Guard your heart. When people say to you something like, "My can you preach! I've never felt such a great anointing before!" stay humble and ask them to keep praying for you. If it's true, then to God be all the glory. You don't deserve any of it. You cannot afford to become proud for any reason. You are nothing, and God is everything, and you want Him to be praised.

When we are involved in any ministry, we must remember that He was the One who called us and gave us the privilege. It is His Church we're ministering to, and we're ministering His Word. Therefore, let all the glory be unto Him.

Having an anointing, being gifted and knowing many scriptures are all wonderful, but they can get you into a lot of trouble with God if you're not careful. Don't let anything start puffing you up.

Some people want to preach so badly, and yet they're so lazy and slothful that they can't be counted upon to do anything else at all in the church. They want to be put on television, when what they really need is to be placed on toilet cleaning duty. After they have cleaned and mopped the church for a while, maybe then they'll be ready for preaching—but not before. They have a lot of humbling and a lot of learning to do first.

ALWAYS RESPECT THE TIME GIVEN TO YOU

One of the ways we show God that we're serious about humility in the ministry and capable of moving higher is to respect the limited time we're given to do anything in public. In any public service, time is limited, and if we monopolize that time just because we're given an opportunity, we probably won't get more opportunities.

In our church, I give one of my people the opportunity to give a few minutes of teaching before the offering in each service, but I purposely limit their time. Why? I want to see if they can be subject to authority. If they do that well, then we can consider some other opportunity for them.

As I was coming up under the apostle, he trained us well in this regard. I became so sensitive to time that I never needed to look at a clock. And, even if I had a limited time, I learned to get my thoughts in and yield the time back to others.

WE DIDN'T HAVE A CLOCK VISIBLE

In our church, we didn't have a clock visible from the pulpit, and if you didn't have a watch, you had to borrow one from someone else. But I never needed one. I just knew when to stop.

"Jones," the pastor would say, "you went exactly fifteen minutes, just like I told you. And you weren't even looking at your watch. How'd you do that?"

"It was the Holy Ghost," I answered, and it was true. I respected the time I was given and asked the Lord to help me stay within it, and He did. When I felt things winding down in my spirit, I knew that it was time to stop.

Many people get so "out of control" that they just have to keep going, passing their assigned time, but the Scriptures declare:

And the spirits of the prophets are subject to the prophets. For God is not the author of confusion, but of peace, as in all churches of the saints.

1 Corinthians 14:32-33

"Nothing's going to hold me back!" some say, but that

person needs to sit down and be quiet. That's the flesh taking over; that's not God. That person is out of control and out of order and needs to be corrected.

"Oh, I feel so good, and the anointing is on me. Let me tell you what the Bible says," they say. The truth is that they should have quit five minutes before, and nothing they say now will be effective.

I HAD TO LEARN IT

This wasn't always so easy and natural for me. Like all other young ministers, I resented it and didn't understand it when we were given only five or ten minutes to speak. That was like teasing to me, for after five or ten minutes, I felt like I was just getting a good start. But the limit on our public time was an important part of our training.

A pastor in Ohio invited me to his church, and when I went, he first asked me just to say something in greeting to his people. The people were blessed by my comments, and began popping up, praising God. When I had sat down, he said, "Would you like to have this young man come and preach for us some time?"

"Yes!" they all answered.

When I was eventually invited to preach in that church, the pastor told me I had thirty minutes. I was disappointed and told my apostle about it. He explained to me how many ministers were trying to take over churches, ignoring the authority of the pastor and riding roughshod over them. Then I understood. The pastor had done the right thing, and I had no reason to be disappointed.

ALWAYS RESPECT SOMEONE ELSE'S HOUSE

When I'm in someone else's church, I am subject to them, and all of us need to learn that very important lesson. In one church, the pastor told me, "Just let the Holy Ghost lead you." Oh, I liked the sound of that. Then he added, "You have ten minutes." That let me know that I was free to let the Spirit lead me within certain bounds, and that was as it should be.

My pastor once told me, "When you conduct a funeral, the family members will require the most unusual things of you, and you have to do what they want. It's their funeral and their loved one, so they're in charge.

"One man asked me to conduct the funeral of his brother who had attended my church," he went on to explain, "and then he limited me to five minutes. I had no choice but to conclude my remarks in the five minutes allotted. It was their funeral, so I had to give them what they wanted. It was their family, so I had to respect their family."

This man was an apostle, but even he could humble himself and respect the needs and feelings of others in their time of pain and suffering. That showed what a great man he was.

When we go into another person's house, we may not agree with them fully, but we must respect them nevertheless. We don't just go in and begin opening up closets or the refrigerator to see what's inside, and we don't move things around without being asked to do so. That's not our house, so we're not free to do whatever we want there.

That night in Ohio, I respected my thirty minutes, and when it was up, I sat down. The pastor got up and said, "This evangelist has been trained right. He knows how to honor another man's house. Now, brother, you can come back, and the next time, we'll give you more time. In fact, preach just as long as you want."

> *When I'm in someone else's church, I am subject to them!*

I hadn't understood why our pastor at the home church was limiting us to five, ten or fifteen minutes. But now I understood. We had to learn to be subject to authority.

"Well, in our church," some say, "we don't do it that way," and they think that justifies them doing something altogether different somewhere else. But when they're in someone else's church, they need to see where they are and respect the authority in that place.

Learn to come under authority everywhere and always. Ministries differ, and more will be expected of you in one place than in another. Learn to adjust, to go with the flow, to obey the local vision. If you insist on forcing your vision upon a local assembly, you will end up causing "di-vision." And you'd better not ever be guilty of that.

MINISTRY REQUIRES HUMILITY

Through the years, God allowed me to see others rebelling against leadership, and all the while, He was preparing me for leadership. I didn't realize that I was being groomed to be a pastor. In fact, I didn't even want to be a pastor. I preferred to be an evangelist, because I saw how pastors were treated, the hurt they had to go through, the pressure they had to bear, and then they had to get up before the people at service times and minister. God was allowing me to see the errors of others so that I would never repeat them myself. We all have a lot to learn.

And the humility we learn doesn't just begin in the pulpit. The humility required for ministry begins at home. If we expect to be used by God, we have to get things straight between husbands and wives, we have to get things straight with our children, and we have to get things straight with whatever leadership we serve under. That's what it means to have a humble spirit, and God honors it every time.

If repentance is needed to restore a relationship, then we need to repent. Someone has to take the lead, so don't wait for the other person to repent. You do it. Have a servant's heart and a humble spirit, and others will follow. The result will be that your ministry is enriched and enlarged. *Humble Is the Way!*

இ

PART V

JESUS AND HUMILITY

CHAPTER 15

OUR SUPREME EXAMPLE

Come unto me, all ye that labour and are heavy laden, and I will give you rest. Take my yoke upon you, and learn of me; for I am meek and lowly in heart: and ye shall find rest unto your souls. For my yoke is easy, and my burden is light. Matthew 11:28-30

Jesus is our example, and He was *"meek and lowly in heart."* That means that He expects us to be *"meek and lowly in heart"* too, and most of us have a long way to go. But that's okay. He invites us to *"come"* and *"learn of [Him]."*

WHAT IT MEANS TO HAVE THE MIND OF CHRIST

This is the very same thing the apostle Paul was trying to say when he told us: *"Let this mind be in you, which was also in Christ Jesus":*

Look not every man on his own things, but every man also on the things of others. Let this mind be in you, which was also in Christ Jesus: who, being in the form of God, thought it not robbery to be equal with God: but made himself of no reputation, and took upon him the form of a servant, and was made in the likeness of men: and being found in fashion as a man, he humbled himself, and became obedient unto death, even the death of the cross. Wherefore God also hath highly exalted him, and given him a name which is above every name: that at the name of Jesus every knee should bow, of things in heaven, and things in earth, and things under the earth; and that every tongue should confess that Jesus Christ is Lord, to the glory of God the Father. Philippians 2:4-11

What kind of *"mind"* are we to have? The mind of Christ. And what was that mind? It was a *"meek"* and *"lowly"* mind, the servant's mind, the attitude of preference for the welfare of others. Jesus laid everything down for us, and we are to do that same thing for each other.

Jesus loved us so much that He chose to make himself *"of no reputation."* He chose to humble Himself and become *"obedient unto death, even the death of the cross."* And did He lose something by demonstrating humility in this way? Not at all. God the Father exalted Him and gave Him a name above all names.

Can you see the direct connection? When Jesus humbled Himself, the Father exalted Him.

WHY WOULD GOD EXALT A STIFFNECKED PERSON?

Why would God exalt a person who was unwilling to receive instruction, reproof or correction? The Bible calls such people *"stiffnecked,"* and God wanted to destroy them in Moses' time:

> *Furthermore the* LORD *spake unto me, saying, I have seen this people, and, behold, it is a stiffnecked people: let me alone, that I may destroy them, and blot out their name from under heaven: and I will make of thee a nation mightier and greater than they.*
>
> Deuteronomy 9:13-14

Why would God exalt a person who was unwilling to receive instruction, reproof or correction?

It was only Moses' intercession that saved the people that day. God is never pleased with pride—wherever it is found.

Jesus chose to die for us, and you must also die—to your will, to your way of thinking, to your ideas. And when you do, you, too, will be exalted. But the dying to self always comes first.

There are many things in our lives that have to die, but we have to want them to die before they can die. For example, never glory in the fact that you still snap at people at the drop of a hat and tell them off. That's not God; it's your flesh! If you'll search deep within your spirit, you'll know when you've done something with a wrong attitude, and if you want to, you can make it right. The goal, of course, is not to always have to correct things after the fact, but to become so humble that you don't do them in the first place.

SEEKING GOD'S HELP TO BE LIKE JESUS

"God, I still have a little vengefulness in me." Have you had to pray that? I've had to talk to God like that. I've said, "God, you know there's still a part of me that wants to fight back, but I know that's not Your will!" He always hears me when I cry out to Him in this way.

If you have a problem with yourself, be honest with God about it. Don't try to keep covering it up. Just admit to God that you're not very humble, and ask Him to help you do what needs to be done. Maybe you'll have to say to God something like this, "Every time my pastor preaches, I find fault with what he says. I'm such a nitpicker that I have to scrutinize every single word. And when I think he's wrong, I make sure he notices that I'm not responding to his message and standing behind him. I'm not humble, Lord. Help me with my self-will!"

Your particular prayer may have other elements, but whatever the content, such prayers never hurt anyone. When you try to change, God's always there to help you. But if you don't even try, then His hands are tied. He's never moved by faithlessness.

If you don't try to change and to become more like

OUR SUPREME EXAMPLE

Jesus, you may be going around this same mountain for the next forty years, accomplishing nothing. Wouldn't it be terrible to get old and still be hateful and mean? When Jesus humbled Himself and became obedient unto death, then God *"highly exalted him,"* and that's what you need too. If you want to get to your next level in God, you must first learn to walk in humility.

You'll Be Tried at Every Step

You can be sure that, like Jesus, you'll be tried at every new level of humility. Through whom will you be tested? Through your spouse, your children, your boss, your pastor, your fellow saints. God will use anyone and everyone.

Do you react humbly when your husband isn't in agreement with what you want to do and insists on having his own way? In the vernacular of the day, do you "have an attitude" or "give an attitude" when you don't get your way? Do you act up in public, not even caring who suddenly knows your business.

You can be walking along one minute, holding hands and looking all googoo-eyed at each other, and then suddenly, because you didn't get your way, you've thrown a little temper tantrum. How sad! Just because you can't agree on everything doesn't mean you should create some public scene. That's not humility; that's flesh. We want people to imitate goodness, righteousness, holiness, meekness and kindness. Our example is Jesus. Can you imagine Him acting like some of us do?

> *The person who wants to be a leader must first learn to be a servant!*

While we're sitting in church, we all believe that we're humble and becoming Christlike. The test comes when we go out to buy something at the store or to get gasoline at the pump. Then the real you shows up. Are you like Jesus yet?

HUMILITY = SERVICE TO OTHERS

One way to know that you're humble and like Jesus is that you prefer others over yourself. You willingly serve. Jesus taught extensively on this subject. For example, He taught:

Ye know that the princes of the Gentiles exercise dominion over them, and they that are great exercise authority upon them. But it shall not be so among you: but whosoever will be great among you, let him be your minister; and whosoever will be chief among you, let him be your servant: even as the Son of man came not to be ministered unto, but to minister, and to give his life a ransom for many. Matthew 20:25-28

If any man desire to be first, the same shall be last of all, and servant of all. Mark 9:35

And whosoever of you will be the chiefest, shall be servant of all. Mark 10:44

He that is the greatest among you shall be your servant. And whosoever shall exalt himself shall be abased; and he that shall humble himself shall be exalted.
Matthew 23:11-12

This is what it means to be humble and Christlike. The person who wants to be a leader must first learn to be a servant. We're not called simply to stand around pointing and telling everyone else what to do. We're called to serve others. People who stand around giving orders to others are nothing but lazy. If you want to be great in the eyes of God, just develop a servant's heart. Then you'll be on your way to becoming truly Christlike.

"LOWER THAN THE ANGELS"

The Scriptures say of Jesus that he was *"made ... a little lower than the angels"*:

HUMBLE IS THE WAY

For thou hast made him a little lower than the angels, and hast crowned him with glory and honour.

Psalm 8:5

Thou madest him a little lower than the angels; thou crownedst him with glory and honour, and didst set him over the works of thy hands: thou hast put all things in subjection under his feet. For in that he put all in subjection under him, he left nothing that is not put under him. But now we see not yet all things put under him. But we see Jesus, who was made a little lower than the angels for the suffering of death, crowned with glory and honour; that he by the grace of God should taste death for every man. Hebrews 2:7-9

What is God trying to say to us when He says that Jesus was made *"a little lower than the angels"*? Angels are immortal; they cannot die, and they do not die. But Jesus, although He was God, had to die. He chose to do this for us, and for that reason, He had to be made *"a little lower than the angels."*

Jesus' choice of mortality made Him vulnerable to hunger and tiredness and other human limitations. He was fully man at the same time He was fully God. But He *was* fully God. He was the great Creator. He was there in the beginning of all things, and without Him nothing was made that was made. In other words, nothing was created without Him. Still, He became willing to humble

180

Himself and live like a man. That took great humility on His part.

Can God die? Absolutely not. That's what's so remarkable about Jesus being willing, not only to die, but also to be beaten by mortal men, to be spit upon by them. His beard was plucked out, and He was so disfigured that He became indistinguishable. The film "The Passion of the Christ" did a lot to make this real to men everywhere. As we watched, it seemed that they would never stop beating Him, and yet Jesus willingly took on that role, and He did it for imperfect creatures like you and me. What humility!

At any moment, Jesus could have breathed on those men and sent them reeling into eternity. At any moment, He could have called for a legion of angels to come and fight for Him and release Him. His restraint was total and complete. He allowed men to capture Him, and He allowed them to torment and kill Him—all because of His great love for us. It was His time to be humble, and He showed us how to do it.

MEEKNESS IS NOT THE SAME AS WEAKNESS

The word *humility* also means "marked by meekness, showing meekness, gentle disposition, submissive," and that sounds like Jesus. But does it sound to you like a weak person? If so, you're wrong. Just because a person is humble, or meek, doesn't mean that they're weak. To the contrary, humility always shows strength. Jesus proved this.

On one occasion, He surprised everyone by taking a whip into the Temple, forcibly overturning the tables of the moneychangers and declaring:

My house shall be called the house of prayer; but ye have made it a den of thieves.   Matthew 21:13

This was the same Jesus who didn't even open His mouth as men tortured and killed Him. So what happened there in the Temple? The zeal of the Lord had *"eaten [Him] up"*:

For the zeal of thine house hath eaten me up; and the reproaches of them that reproached thee are fallen upon me.   Psalm 69:9

The moneychangers must have been startled that day. The Man who approached them seemed to be much more than a mere man, and He was speaking for God, as if He were God Himself. And, of course, He was God wrapped in human flesh. That must have been a scary moment for those men who made their living by taking advantage of the Temple worshippers. They probably never forgot it. Later, that same Jesus bowed His head and allowed mere men to take His life. That's humility, and He left us a supreme example to follow.

OUR SUPREME EXAMPLE

OUR CALL TO FOLLOW JESUS

Jesus was the Son of the living God, and yet He willingly became the servant of all for our sake. Can you imagine it? He allowed the very men He had created to abuse and kill Him.

He has called us to be servants, and when we can no longer serve, it's an indication that pride has taken control of us. Refusing to give of yourself for the benefit of others shows exactly where your heart is. Jesus did not come *"to be ministered unto, but to minister, and to give His life for a ransom for many."* Are you like Jesus yet? *Humble Is the Way!*

CHAPTER 16

ADOPTING JESUS' EXAMPLE

The LORD shall fight for you, and ye shall hold your peace.   Exodus 14:14

There are many things we can learn from the short life of Jesus on earth and then adopt as part of our own way of life. We call ourselves Christians, and that means like Christ, so this is a worthwhile way to grow spiritually.

Therefore take a close look at Jesus. He's the Master, the very Son of God. Would He say what you're saying? Would He do what you're doing? If Jesus wouldn't say it, then you shouldn't be saying it either, and if He wouldn't be doing it, then you shouldn't be doing it either. The classic question, *What Would Jesus Do?,* is still valid today.

JESUS COULD HOLD HIS PEACE

One of the things we can learn from Jesus was His ability to hold His peace when others provoked Him. Of course He had Almighty God and all the angels of Heaven behind Him, but so do you.

Being humble means learning to hold your peace and let God fight your battles, but most of us can't yet do that. If you'll just hold your peace, God will defend you and avenge you, but that seems to be a big "IF."

Some might say, "Pastor, I've never seen God avenge me." Well, do you ever hush up long enough to give Him the chance? Do you ever just stop talking and wait to see what He'll do? I've found, as I've walked with God, that our battle must be a "hushed-mouth" battle. Let me explain what I mean by that. Many times you're right, and you could say something, but you choose not to. Instead, you let God defend you.

Don't you ever get tired of putting your foot in your mouth?

For some of us, that's very hard. We feel that we just have to say something. It's itching in our feet, and we just have to give someone a piece of our mind. As the saying goes, you'd better keep that little piece; you might need it tomorrow.

"But I have to tell them something!" some people protest. "You don't know what they did to me."

But why do you have to tell them? Why can't you just let God tell them? Why don't you let Him speak into their ear? Things are not working out your way anyway, and if it's not working, why pursue it? If things are not working your way, then it's time to do things God's way, and His way is the way of humility.

JUST WALK AWAY

Don't you ever get tired of putting your foot in your mouth? You know in your mind what you want to say, but when you actually get around to saying it, it doesn't come out like you wanted it to. But all the while God has been saying, "Just hold your peace."

Didn't you hear Him? God says, "Hold your peace," so don't stand there and keep looking the person in the eyes. Just turn and walk away.

Just walk away! That's right, just walk away! It's as simple as that.

If you walk away, all argument is ended. That person won't stand there arguing with themselves. If you walk away, the issue is resolved.

"Where are you going?" they might ask.

Just answer them, "I'm keeping peace."

If they ask, "How's that?" tell them, "We're both 'hot heads' right now, and if we continue to argue, I'm going to disrespect you, or you're going to disrespect me. So let's let things cool off for a while. We can talk about it later."

If they try to insist, tell them, "Give me time to cool off a little. I don't want to miss God and get out of His will. I don't want to say the wrong thing." Insist on doing it God's way, and that's the way of humility.

No Peace!

Many times we have no peace about a situation, and it's because we're not doing things God's way. We're suffering the consequences of our disobedience and rebellion, and part of those consequences is to have no peace and no contentment.

Some of us are so headstrong that we insist on doing it our way. "I'm going to do it. I'm going to say it. And I don't care what anyone says or does—even God!"

Okay! Well, be ready to pay the price for your hardness of heart and stubbornness. You'll have no peace and no contentment in your soul as a result.

Do you realize that everything would be different in your life if you learned how to hold your peace? Why is it that you always have to say something?

Our Big Mouths Get Us into So Much Trouble

While we were growing up, my mother would be correcting my sister, giving her godly instruction, and my sister would tell her she didn't want to hear it. "All right, young lady," Mother would answer, "you don't want to hear it from me, but one day you'll have to hear it from God." Her words surely came to pass. In time, my sister had to go through Hell—all because she refused to hear instruction.

She was very intelligent, very beautiful and very quick thinking, and she was sure she could outthink and out-talk any man. But many men won't suffer that from a woman, and the men in her life invariably turned on her with brute force. She suffered the consequences of never being willing to hold her peace.

I once heard a man of God prophesying over a group of women, telling them that God would fight for them—if they would just learn to hold their peace. "You're always wondering why you have to keep picking yourself up off the floor," he said. "It's because you refuse to hold your tongue. You're provoking your husbands."

He was not saying that what was happening to them was right; he was just telling them why it was happening. If they could learn to hold their tongue, he said, they would radically change their situations.

When he said that, one lady started screaming. That word had touched her heart, and you can be sure that God was ready to avenge her.

SILENCE BRINGS ITS REWARDS

One of my pastors once told me about a Christian woman whose husband was not saved. When she would go to church in the winter time, he would lock her out of the house so that she couldn't get back in. She would have to stand on the porch pleading with him to let her in from the cold. He made her suffer in this way just because she wanted to serve God.

When the church people heard about it, some of the brothers wanted to get bats and go take care of that man, but they did the wise thing and left him in the hands of God.

That husband continued to fight his wife tooth and nail about going to church, and that wife kept right on loving him and praying for him. The next thing they knew the man was eaten up with cancer and died. Then the woman was able to live in peace and serve God the way she wanted to. Humility is the way to accomplish everything.

IT TAKES TWO TO TANGO

When we counsel with couples in distress, there are always two sides to the story. Usually, we let the woman speak first, and she has her version of things. Then, we hear the other side. It is only after we hear both sides that the whole truth begins to become apparent.

There are always two sides to the story because it takes two to tango. When you go to wash your hands, both of them have to cooperate, or it's a very difficult process. Try washing with just one hand without the help of the other. It's a chore. In fact, it's practically impossible.

Newton's Law of physics states that "to every action there's an equal and opposite reaction," and it relates to our interactions in marriage as well as physics.

"Pastor, he told me to 'shut up,' " some women say.

"Well, why would he tell you that? Was it because you just kept on talking?"

"Yes," she has to admit.

And that's the problem. Insult feeds on insult, and violence feeds on violence. We all need to learn to hold our peace.

DON'T BE SO EAGER

Don't be so eager to jump on someone when they say something you don't like. Other people are not the problem; you're the problem. If you're too quick to react, it may signify that there are some wounds in you that haven't yet been healed. They're still raw, and when someone strikes a nerve, it can set you off. So, watch what you say. The Scriptures warn us:

> *There are always two sides to the story!*

> For by thy words thou shalt be justified, and by thy words thou shalt be condemned.   Matthew 12:37

If you insist on saying exactly what you want to say, you can do it. But you'll pay a heavy price.

You don't have to always have the last say. You don't

have to always be right. Why not be humble for once? You don't have to speak out what you're thinking, especially when you know it will only cause dissention and add fuel to the fire. If you think before you speak, often you'll realize that every time you say something critical, the situation just deteriorates further. So, it's obvious that you're just making things worse. Keep silent, and give things time to heal.

Sometimes you win with silence. If you can just hold your peace, God will work. Say to Him, "God, I'm going to let You fight this battle for me. I'm always trying to defend myself, always trying to prove myself, always trying to show that I'm right and the other person is wrong. Now, I give You the right to intervene on my behalf." That's the humble way, and God will reward it.

God said that if you would just hold your peace, He would fight for you. But that's conditional. What He does depends on what you do.

STOP PUSHING GOD ASIDE

Many Christians have been in church for twenty years or more and never once seen the Lord taking a stand for them. In all that time, they've never seen God bring them out of a situation. And the reason is that they're always pushing Him out of the way and trying to take care of every situation themselves. You just need to step back and say, "Lord, handle this for me. I'm tired of my flesh getting in the way of progress in You. I keep failing these tests, and I know it's not Your will."

It's time to hold your peace, and the Spirit of God is speaking to us, saying those simple words: "Hold your peace!"

"But I just have to say it!"

"Hold your peace!"

That's pride that makes you want to speak up. The moment you feel that you just have to say something, that's pride at work. Put it in its place.

Sometimes, it almost seems that we're intoxicated with the need to prove that we're right. We're on some kind of high, and it's nothing more than pride at work. Humble yourself! And stop pushing God aside.

RIGHT OR WRONG, HUMBLE YOURSELF

Nothing beats humility. Whether you're right or wrong, stay humble. Sometimes you can be absolutely right, but your timing in telling someone is all wrong. Hold your peace and wait on the Lord, and you will see His hand move.

Our impulse is to take care of the matter. Why wait? That's why some never see the hand of God at work for them. How could they? They don't give Him a chance. Wait for the proper time or let God take care of the matter in His own way.

We justify ourselves in speaking out because we're right, but if our right comment is out of sync, out of time, it just won't work. It will only make things worse. Hold your peace and let God fight for you. Hold your peace, and let Him show Himself strong on your behalf. *Humble Is the Way!*

CHAPTER 17

How Can You Get Humble
and Stay Humble?

HUMBLE YOURSELVES in the sight of the Lord, and
he shall lift you up.   James 4:10, Emphasis added

HUMBLE YOURSELVES therefore under the mighty
hand of God, that he may exalt you in due time.
                                    1 Peter 5:6, Emphasis added

"He shall lift you up!" I like that, don't you? *"That he*
may exalt you in due time." That's what I want, don't you?
So we have no problem and no difference of opinion
about what we want in life, but how do we get there?
That's the problem. How can we become humble and
stay humble?

You Have to Humble Yourself

Wouldn't it be wonderful if we could all take a humble
pill and instantly become humble or enhance our exist-

ing humility? But God could never permit that. This is something He insists that you have do yourself. No one else can do it for you—not even God Himself.

Oh yes, God can humble you, and He will if He has to. But, believe me, that's not the way you want to achieve humility. Just ask Ananias and Sapphira, Saul, Uzziah and the millions of others who have insisted on doing it the hard way. God says, *"Humble yourself!"* And that's the way He wants it done.

Humble, as a verb, means "to bring under subjection." And that's exactly what you have to do with your flesh before God and before man. You have to talk to it, take authority over it and bring it down. God won't do it for you; you have to do it for yourself. It's your flesh, so no one else can control it. You're the only one with that authority.

What Few Seem to Understand

This is the part of humility that many don't seem to understand. They keep waiting around, hoping for humility, praying for humility and believing for humility, but humility never comes that way. You can pray from now until you breathe your last breath on earth, and God's answer will still be the same: *"Humble yourself!"* You can quote every scriptural promise and declare it over your life and then do it again and again, but the answer will always be the same: *"Humble yourself."* This message will never change, because there simply is no other way.

Unless you take authority over your own flesh and bring it into line, it simply won't be done. So if you have to do it yourself, then you'd better start learning how to do it. Otherwise, you'll live out your life in frustration and go to an early grave.

It's not wrong to pray that God will help you with humility, but don't sit around waiting for Him to make you humble. *"Humble yourself."* Without humility, you cannot have a proper relationship with God and with man, and this is the only way to achieve humility: *"Humble yourself."*

THE FIRST KEY TO ACHIEVING HUMILITY

So, what's the key to achieving humility? Although God demands that you *"humble yourself,"* He knows that you're actually powerless to do it in your own strength, so He willingly provides you the necessary power. Just before His return to Heaven, the promise of the Lord to His disciples was this:

God knows that you're actually powerless to humble yourself in your own strength, so He willingly provides you the necessary power!

But ye shall receive power, after that the Holy Ghost is come upon you: and ye shall be witnesses unto me both in Jerusalem, and in all Judaea, and in Samaria, and unto the uttermost part of the earth.   Acts 1:8

Yes, this Holy Ghost power promised by the Lord is for evangelizing the world. It's for preaching the Gospel, casting out demons and healing the sick. But if we don't first use God's power to humble ourselves, we'll never get to the other things.

If we, as believers, are not going to use God's power, why should He give it to us in the first place? He has given us His power, and it has a purpose. It is to make us overcomers.

The Holy Ghost, our Comforter, is present to help us and to assist us. One of His names, Paracletos (or Paraclete) means, "one called alongside to assist." He's there in your life, so let Him work.

A Second Key to Achieving Humility

Another key to overcoming flesh and pride is to *"put on the Lord Jesus Christ."* This robs the flesh of its power:

But put ye on the Lord Jesus Christ, and make not provision for the flesh, to fulfil the lusts thereof.
Romans 13:14

The choice is clear. We can let the flesh have its way,

or we can deny the flesh its victory. *"Make not provision for the flesh."*

Some people insist, "That's just my way, Pastor. I've always been like that. When anyone says something unkind to me, I've always been quick to snap at them." Okay, maybe that's true. That's your way of doing things, but is it the way of the Lord? It's time that you abandon your ways and adopt His ways.

EXPECTING CHANGE

When we come to God, there are things that fall off of us very quickly, there are other things that take time for us to conquer, and there are still other things that we seem to struggle with forever. The reason is that there is a part of us that wants to keep these things around. We're not fully cooperating with God's Spirit in ridding ourselves of these things, and so they stubbornly cling to us.

Stop insisting that this is just the way you are and this is just the way you'll always be. You can change—by adopting the ways of Christ and denying your flesh its pleasures.

But you'll never change unless you want to. You have to make up your mind that you want to change, and then you have to force your flesh to cooperate with that change. If you're a believer, God has already given you power to do that. Your power, the power God has given you, is not just over the devil and his imps; it's also over you yourself, over your own flesh.

What is this *dunamis* power that we have for, if not to help us overcome our stubborn flesh? As we have noted, some think that it's only power to go forth and preach, but how can you go forth and preach to others, if you can't first get victory over yourself?

You have conquering power, and the first thing you need to conquer is your own flesh!

You have conquering power, and the first thing you need to conquer is your own flesh. Put it under right now before it puts you under.

Force your flesh to do the right thing—whether it likes it or not (and it won't). Everything going on around you will work to set your flesh off, but you have to insist on turning control over to the Holy Ghost, submitting yourself to His will for your life and making your flesh tow the line.

This means that we're to stop making excuses for our wrong behavior. Don't worry if the other party is doing their part or not. The important thing is: are you doing your part? That's where we get into trouble. We're trying to fix or correct the other party, but God wants to correct us. They're not the problem; we are. You need to deal with *you,* and don't worry about whether the other party is treating you right or not. How are you treating them?

HOW CAN YOU GET HUMBLE AND STAY HUMBLE?

Are You Humble Yet?

Are you humble? Just because a person is quiet doesn't mean that they're humble. They may not be saying anything out loud, but their body language does not agree. I had a friend like that. He was always very quiet, and when we asked him why, he said that he was just checking everybody else out. Later we learned that he was very sneaky and was constantly trying to swindle other people.

Quietness doesn't necessarily indicate humility. Instead, there must be some visible fruit of humility: patience, gentleness and longsuffering. When a submitted person resists the devil, he flees. A proud person opens every door to him.

So, stop making excuses for your bad behavior, and humble yourself.

"But you don't know how they ..."

What I do know is that God requires humility on our part.

"But ..."

Just humble yourself!

Are you humble? That's the important question. Humble is the way.

Paul Brought His Own Body Under Subjection

To *humble* is "to afflict; to make meek; to bring the body under subjection." Paul said:

But I keep under my body, and bring it into subjection: lest that by any means, when I have preached to others, I myself should be a castaway.

1 Corinthians 9:27

Too many times we're not at all concerned about bringing ourselves under subjection. Instead, we're concerned about how best to tell someone off. That's not God; that's flesh. And those who operate in the flesh are doomed to destruction:

For if ye live after the flesh, ye shall die: but if ye through the Spirit do mortify the deeds of the body, ye shall live. Romans 8:13

We need to mortify the deeds of the flesh, and mortify means to kill. So kill that flesh. Tell yourself: "You're going to fall into line. You will love, and you will be quick to forgive. You will not harbor anything in your heart, and you will do what's right." We have power and authority over the devil and over ourselves, and therefore we have the authority to do this.

Too often we fail to use the power we have—at least in the right way. We're quick to use it on someone else, but slow to use it on ourselves. Bring your creature under subjection, for God won't do it for you.

SEEK GOD WITH YOUR WHOLE HEART

The psalmist learned to seek God with his *"whole heart"*:

HOW CAN YOU GET HUMBLE AND STAY HUMBLE?

With my whole heart have I sought thee; O let me not wander from thy commandments.   Psalm 119:10

There should be something in you that makes you want to go to church. There should be something tugging at you, making you want to seek God.

Jesus told us the same thing, when He said:

Seek ye first the kingdom of God ... , and all these things shall be added unto you.   Matthew 6:33

Men and women of today do just the opposite. They go running after things first. Jesus is beckoning to us, telling us of His love and urging us to come to Him, and we keep running after things. The result is that we struggle in our flesh to get things done and can't, and we end up blaming God, thinking that His promises are not true. It's time to put flesh in its place and seek God wholeheartedly.

FLESH WILL NEVER DO THE RIGHT THING

Our flesh never wants to lower itself, and it's never ready to submit to the will of another. Something in our nature makes us always want to be number one. This tendency to pride and rebelliousness is in all of us from earliest childhood. If you give a child candy one day and the next day you say to them, "You can't have any candy today," you'll soon see that flesh rise. It's there.

You have to make your flesh mind. You have to make

yourself meek, and it won't happen any other way. You're the only one who can do it, for no one else has power over you.

PETER ON HUMILITY

Peter had much more to say to the Church about mutual submission:

> *Likewise, ye younger, submit yourselves unto the elder. Yea, all of you be subject one to another, and be clothed with humility: for God resisteth the proud, and giveth grace to the humble. Humble yourselves therefore under the mighty hand of God, that he may exalt you in due time: casting all your care upon him; for he careth for you.* 1 Peter 5:5-7

Who was this message to? *"All of you."*
And what are we all to do? *"Be clothed with humility."*
It's time to take off those garments of pride and put on humility. It's something YOU have to do. Put it on. Make yourself bow before Jesus. Make yourself love others. Make yourself forgive those who have offended you. If you don't do it, who will?

If Jesus humbled Himself, then we have no excuse. He was tempted by pride, just as we are, but He humbled Himself. So drop the phony excuses and start making your spirit do the right thing. Humble yourself. No one else can do it for you. Only you have that power. *Humble Is the Way!*

᷾

EPILOGUE

I wouldn't want to leave you, precious reader, with the impression that I have somehow arrived at perfection in this regard. Believe me, I haven't. Achieving the humility we all desire is an ongoing process—whatever our status in the Church or our years of knowing the Lord. I'm never bothered if a member says to me, "Pastor, I'm not sure that I'm humble yet." I know just what they're saying. They have achieved some degree of humility, but they want more.

And that's the important thing. You may not be very humble yet, but do you want to be? If you want to be, you will be, for it's your will that controls the process. One day I know that I will be able to say with Jesus, *"I am meek and lowly in heart,"* and I thank my God that He has prepared the journey necessary to get me there.

In the interest of keeping this book short enough for the average reader, we have not yet touched on exciting subjects like Humility and Forgiveness, Humility and Giving, Humility and Prayer and Humility and Worship. Perhaps these will fill the pages of a future volume. This subject is inexhaustible and its impact on our daily lives great. The words *pride, proud* and *proudly* are used in the Bible more than a hundred times, and the words *humble, humbled, humbleth, humbledst* and *humility* are used nearly seventy times. God has a lot to say on this subject, and we're just beginning to learn. *Humble Is the Way!*

∽

— NOTES —

Ministry Page

To contact Pastor David Jones, use any of the following:

House of Praise
P.O. Box 843
Katy, Texas 77492-0843

Phone: 832-863-5927
E-mail: houseofpraise@houseofpraiseinternational.org
Web site: www.houseofpraiseinternational.org

CPSIA information can be obtained at www.ICGtesting.com
Printed in the USA
BVOW020405180712

295518BV00001B/137/P